MY TEACHER,
MY SON

Praise for *My Teacher, My Son*

"It seems impossible that a book about unimaginable grief could offer so much hope, yet that is the gift of *My Teacher, My Son*. With breathtaking honesty, Nick Shaw shows how love, joy, and continued connection co-exist with loss, change, and challenge. The courage of Nick's self-reflection empowers each of us to find a way forward. A truly heart-empowering read."

Kelly McGonigal, PhD
Research Psychologist, Stanford University Lecturer, and Author of *The Joy of Movement: How Exercise Helps Us Find Happiness, Hope, Connection, and Courage*

"As a father and a skier, I found that this book — this compelling, tragic, yet somehow deeply uplifting story — holds your heart from the moment you meet Nick and his family, and it never lets go. Sadly, as a person present on February 19, 2019, I knew too well the outcome of events. But what I wasn't prepared for in reading *My Teacher, My Son* was encountering the depth of paternal and familial love that came later. Nick has taught me about the depth of human resilience, and how much we can learn and grow even from an unimaginable loss."

Taylor Middleton
President and COO, Big Sky Resorts

"With gripping intensity, Nick Shaw shares the terror of losing his nine-year-old son in an accident on a mountain after sharing a much-anticipated summit ski. Nick is determined to investigate his grief in a way that maintains a loving connection to his son and serves as an example to readers of his powerful memoir, *My Teacher, My Son*. Fueled by the knowledge that things can change in a moment, he calls on us to pause and be with the complex terrain of grief; he inspires us to move into the strength that comes from exploring our vulnerability so we may ultimately become more present in our lives. While healing is not linear and is deeply personal, Nick courageously shares his journey so we all feel less alone with unimaginable loss."

Nancy Rappaport, MD
Associate Professor of Psychiatry, Harvard Medical School; Author of *The Behavior Code: A Practical Guide to Understanding and Teaching the Most Challenging Students* and *In Her Wake: A Child Psychiatrist Explores the Mystery of Her Mother's Suicide*

"This heart-piercing book is a tragic story, authentically and beautifully told. Nick Shaw brings the reader into deep resonance with the entire arc of his experience, with precise sharing of all the emotions — panic, pain, despair, yearning — all the understandable ruminations and all his efforts to reach again for joy, connection, and meaning. It is a short read but an intensely impactful story that bravely reminds every one of us to learn from loss, deal with our demons, make life matter, and focus on love above all else."

Michelle Brody, PhD
Executive Coach, Clinical Psychologist, and Author of *Stop the Fight! An Illustrated Guide for Couples* and *Own Your Armor: Revolutionary Change for Workplace Culture*

"In this gripping and emotionally raw account of losing his son in a ski accident, Nick Shaw takes us on a rollercoaster of unimaginable shock and sorrow. In seeking to find meaning and make sense of the tragedy, Nick shares his spiritual journey and the creative process that has helped him heal, stay connected to William, and strive for a sense of calmness and serenity. Nick's degree of vulnerability in *My Teacher, My Son* is a testament to his courage and a reminder to us all to embrace our emotions and be in the moment so we can open the path to personal growth and healing."

Suki Gill
Co-Founder of Mirrorbox Leadership Lab

"How is it possible to simultaneously hate that this is a true story and love that Nick Shaw wrote it for us? Powerful, gut-wrenching, inspired, and optimistic. *My Teacher, My Son* is poetic and poignant, with universal lessons and thought-provoking discussions about what it means to be our best selves in an unpredictable world."

Kate Colbert
Speaker, Communications Coach, Publishing Professional, and Author of *Think Like a Marketer: How a Shift in Mindset Can Change Everything for Your Business* and *Commencement: The Beginning of a New Era in Higher Education*

"The death of a child is an unimaginable tragedy. In his powerful memoir, *My Teacher, My Son*, Nick Shaw bares his soul in a poignant, courageous, heartbreaking, and remarkably heart-forward way. He shares how he is evolving and growing through loss, vulnerability, connections, and the love lessons that follow. It's not a straight line, nor can it ever be."

Jenny Kaplan, PhD, LICSW
Founder, Jeff's Place and FRIENDS Way, and Author of *You Are Not Alone: Young Adults Coping with Death*

MY TEACHER, MY SON

Lessons on Life, Loss, and Love

NICK SHAW

SnowGlobe
PUBLISHING

Published by SnowGlobe Publishing (Carlisle, MA)

Editing by:
Kate Colbert

Cover design and typesetting by:
George Stevens

First edition, November 2023
Paperback ISBN: 979-8-9882590-2-2
Hardcover ISBN: 979-8-9882590-7-7

Library of Congress Control Number: 2023915829
Created in the United States of America

About the Cover:
The Shaw children — whose lives inspired their father, Nick Shaw, to write this remarkable and raw account of life, loss, and love — were given names with powerful meanings, each of which is represented on the cover of this book. The wolf represents William; the sea represents Kai; the tree represents Bodhi.

BE YOURSELF!

How Readers of *My Teacher, My Son* Pay It Forward to Tomorrow's Children

A portion of the proceeds from the retail sales of *My Teacher, My Son* will be donated to William's Be Yourself Challenge (WBYC), a 501c3 nonprofit organization established in honor of William Wolfgang Shaw. WBYC works to help kids find the courage to be their authentic selves and is dedicated to educating parents, teachers and kids on important mental health topics, providing opportunities for kids to express themselves through movement, and building community through connection and service.

Dedication

For my greatest teachers, William, Kai, and Bodhi.

And for my wife, Susie — my partner and soul mate on this journey.

Table of Contents

Prologue xiii

Introduction 1

Chapter 1   The Moments 8

Chapter 2   Four Words 24

Chapter 3   To Be Seen by a Stranger 30

Chapter 4   The Missing Seat 36

Chapter 5   W.W.W.W. 48

Chapter 6   Love Manifest 54

Chapter 7   What If? 64

Chapter 8   Polarities 70

Chapter 9   The Pride of a Father, the Pride of a Son 78

Chapter 10   The Wolf's Path 88

Chapter 11   The Resilience of the Sea 96

Chapter 12   Bodhisattva 104

Chapter 13   The Last Thought 110

Epilogue 117

My Wish for You 122

Acknowledgments 125

About the Author 129

Go Beyond the Book 133

Keep In Touch 135

Prologue

By Susie Shaw

MY HUSBAND, NICK, and I are complimentary. This is a nice way to say that we're the proverbial "opposites who attract."

I say *yes* to everything and everyone. Nick's first response is always *no* ... and, eventually, he may come around to *yes* (with enough prodding or enough time).

I am outgoing, an extrovert, an over-sharer. Nick, on the other hand, rarely opens up to others. He's an introvert and feels most fulfilled from a quiet night at home with his closest friends and family.

Nick told me recently that I "talk to think" and he "thinks to talk." That sounds about right. I process feelings and experiences by sitting down with friends and family, rolling over detail after detail, crying and laughing and then crying again. I am one who "thinks out loud." In sharp contrast, when Nick is feeling overwhelmed, anxious, or is grappling with a tough emotion, I can usually find him in a quiet space — alone and delving deep inside himself. Nick thinks in silence.

But life being what it is — messy, complicated, unexpected — there's always that one moment that's a deviation from the usual ... an exception to the rule. Sometimes we think, feel, and behave in a way that is outside our default state. This book — this story — is not Nick's "usual." It's his *extraordinary*.

Back before we had kids and still had the energy to head out for dinner and drinks, Nick would always order a vodka soda. Simple, brief, neat, and clean. This book is like Nick sidling up to the bar and ordering a tequila sunrise with a shot of whiskey on the side. Complicated and complex, so hard to swallow, leaving a burning feeling in your heart. Every word of this book is so out of character for Nick. Even as his wife, I can't quite imagine how hard it was for him to step out of his comfort zone in this way, to allow readers to see the most beautiful display of vulnerability and self-awareness he could possibly write. I'm so proud of him for saying "yes" to writing this book and doing it in such a raw, emotional, and powerful way. William's death forced Nick to veer in a new direction and, for the first time in his life, Nick felt compelled to share all his fears, all his insecurities, and all his wisdom. Here, in *My Teacher, My Son*, my remarkable husband has stepped away from his usual safe and familiar pattern and has instead chosen to share it all. How terribly lucky we all are.

In our family, Nick has always been the rock. He is a safe harbor in our individual and collective storms. He is steadfast and loyal and is the ultimate listener. Nick spent his childhood listening to his father philosophize, to his mother psychoanalyze, and to his siblings tell tales of their elaborate escapades. Through all the chatter in his New York City apartment, Nick just took it all in. He was an insecure kid, and often felt intimidated to share himself in front of such confident personalities. Eventually, he capitalized on this unique skill of acute listening and built a successful career as an executive coach. His job is to listen to other people's stories — other people's challenges at work and in life. He was always going to be great in this role, and tragically he has become so much better since losing his son. When William died, the strong and steady countenance that Nick always presented was cracked wide open. All his fears and his anxieties were finally exposed to the light. William's death opened his eyes to so many of life's possibilities — the possibilities and lessons we all miss when we're moving too fast. William's death forced Nick to slow down and to allow the pain and suffering to transform his outlook on just how beautiful life can be. Nick tapped into his superpower as a gifted listener and has been able to hear what others often cannot — the whisperings of a son on the other side. Lessons from William, his continual teacher and guide.

Life — and death — will teach us at every turn. When I was in design school in my late 20s, I had a teacher named Tommy Yamamoto. Tommy was an architectural renderer — an artist who produced the most captivating paintings of buildings for his clients. I took a watercolor rendering class with Tommy where he taught the art of creating shadows. I can still hear Tommy exclaim that we have "no choice" as to where we put our shadows. The sun only allows shadows to fall in one way from an object. The light and the dark are predetermined by the larger force of the sun, and we can only follow its course when designing a space or creating a painting. I believe that Nick and I, in the wake of William's death, had no choice but to follow the path we are on — the path of lightness over dark, truth over containment. We are driven by a force larger than ourselves, perhaps the force of William himself, urging us on toward the light from his place in the universe. Each time we feel the shadows creeping in, again and again we only have one choice as we continue to move forward. That choice is love.

> **I believe that Nick and I, in the wake of William's death, had no choice but to follow the path we are on — the path of lightness over dark, truth over containment.**

Looking back on our last night together in Montana, it seems to me that the universe was already laying the groundwork for what was to come. On the eve of a big skiing adventure, we were supposed to have dinner with our friends, the Svateks, at Riverhouse — a BBQ joint on the banks of the Gallatin River in Big Sky. We headed into town early to get the boys new goggles at the local outdoor gear shop. As the boys were trying out the latest styles, we received a phone call from the Svateks. Despite their best efforts, they couldn't get their car out of the parking lot. They had regrettably gotten a rental car without 4-wheel drive and the tires were so bald that it couldn't make it up the small incline at the exit from their vacation condo. So rather than dining as a group of eight, we ended up eating — just the four of us (me, Nick, William, and Kai) — at the local brewery. There, William tried buffalo chicken wings for the first time and loved them. We have a picture of him, his fingers and face stained from the signature orange sauce, a grin from ear to ear. I remember that dinner so vividly, and it's particularly special because it wasn't supposed to happen — not that restaurant, not that menu, not that group of people. It hadn't been part of our plan. We were slated to have a big, boisterous group dinner, and it turned into our last dinner as a family of four ... because the universe needed it that way. Because that simple memory would need to last us a lifetime.

The night before.

Our lifetime together, in fact, began by happenstance. Nick and I met on a blind date in Manhattan. We were randomly thrown together, and yet it was a perfect fit from the start. Time and time again, the trajectory of our lives as a couple would defy the odds. When we were hoping to have children, doctors told us I'd have a hard time conceiving. Yet William came to us unplanned and unexpected — a perfect gift. I often wonder about what my life would have looked like had I not met Nick that spring night in 2002. Could I have escaped the excruciating pain of losing a nine-year-old child if I had met and married someone else? Would I have walked through life without the burden of immense grief that I will always carry now? I've come to answer these questions with a resounding *no*. No — simply because I no longer wish away the pain and grief like I did when William first died. I wouldn't trade one second with William for a life free from heartache. I would choose the privilege of being William's mom again and again, knowing the devastating end that would befall him. I was destined to be Nick's wife; I was destined to be William's mom.

I would choose the privilege of being William's mom again and again, knowing the devastating end that would befall him. I was destined to be Nick's wife; I was destined to be William's mom.

Where we stand today, this is the way it's supposed to happen. I am here to lovingly raise Kai and Bodhi despite our sadness, and Nick is here to teach us all how to find truth and meaning in a world marred by tragedy and challenge.

I have a story to tell too, but here — right now in this remarkable book he has written for you — this is Nick's story.

I love you, Nick. You know I do.

Introduction

I HAVE THREE sons — William, Kai, and Bodhi.

On February 19, 2019, my family suffered the unbearable. What started out as a magical day — skiing at Big Sky, Montana — ended in the tragic death of my oldest son, William. He was nine years old.

In the days after William's death, amidst the fog of deep grief, the phrase "my teacher, my son" came to me in a moment of clarity. In that instant, I realized that William had been teaching me powerful lessons since the day he was born. When we buried William's ashes at Green Cemetery in our hometown of Carlisle, Massachusetts, I read a poem that I had written as a tribute to him. It best captures the impact that his short life and death has had on me.

> My teacher, my son ...
> At birth, you taught me to live my truth.
> In life, you taught me the beauty of imperfection.
> In death, you taught me the power of love.

Our kids, if we are open to it, can be amazing teachers. When you hold a child for the first time, you feel a kind of love that is so visceral it over-whelms. When I first held William, I remember looking down at him and not being able to take my eyes off him. Here was this tiny and beautiful new life that Susie and I had created. His hair, which would eventually turn blond, was jet black, and his slightly jaundiced skin made him look sun-kissed. He shared my dark features, and it felt as if I were looking at myself in a mirror from my past. For the first time in a long time, a feeling of wonder flowed through my entire body. *Who is this tiny being I am holding? Who will he be when he grows up? How can I be the best possible father to him along his journey?*

To Have Loved and Lost

I have learned that when you lose a child, your love for them is magnified exponentially. You long not only for what *was* but for what *could have been*. As I felt the pull of so many memories — his first steps, the silly games we played, that time he broke his hand while skateboarding — and as I looked into the void of the future, I felt a pain so intense I almost couldn't go on. Even at its worst, that pain is love in its rawest form and — in the very manifestation of the word "bittersweet" — no matter how bad my emotional pain became, I still wanted to hold onto it. Because the sum of excruciatingly beautiful memories was the thread connecting me to the little boy I had lost.

> **I have learned that when you lose a child, your love for them is magnified exponentially. You long not only for what *was* but for what *could have been*.**

Eventually, I learned that the intensity of the pain subsides, and that love manifests in other places. In the days and months after William's death, we experienced countless acts of love from our family, friends, and community. Our instincts took over and we focused the love we had for William on our younger son, Kai, to make sure he would be OK and that we would remain intact as a family. As our family healed, this love manifested once again when our youngest son, Bodhi, was born a year and half after William's accident.

In the months after William died, I had a strong need to make meaning out of something that seemed so random and senseless. For me, that meaning-making process was about learning from this tragedy so that I could live and experience this life differently. Every morning, I would go into William's room, with the hope of finding some way to connect with him so that he could guide me through my discovery journey. I would sit — initially on William's green bunk bed and then on the day bed that we replaced it with — and meditate. As I settled into a calm state, I would silently ask, "What lessons can be learned from this?" I listened between breaths. Sometimes I heard nothing but silence; sometimes ideas and thoughts would come to me from the depths of my subconsciousness. Once my meditation was finished, I would grab my black leather journal, first observing how my grief was impacting me and then making note of any lessons that came to me in my meditation. Lastly, I would write a letter to William and share with him where I was.

Fresh Perspectives from Fresh Tragedy

One of the gifts that tragedy can bring is to offer you a different perspective on life. Most of us tend to get lost in the hustle and bustle of daily life and fail to focus on what really matters. Before William's death, I certainly was on that path as my focus on career began to dominate all my time and attention. In contemplating William's life in the aftermath of losing him, I realized that his birth inspired me to grapple with my own life more honestly.

William was our first child. When he was born, I was 34 years old and working hard as the Director of Business Process at Otis Spunkmeyer, a cookie company in San Leandro, California. As I contemplated fatherhood in the months before and after William's birth, it dawned on me that he was going to look to me to be his model for what it meant to be a man and a father. It was an overwhelming responsibility and, at the same time, a profound gift of opportunity. I was frustrated and depressed in a career that did not fulfill me. I knew I was unhappy but, without a clear sense of what was the next right step, I was stuck.

Stepping into my new sense of fatherhood, several months after William's birth I realized that I couldn't be in a career that I wasn't even remotely passionate about. What would that signal to William? Wanting to be a good teacher and role model now that I was a father, I finally broke free from the years-long continuous cycle of feeling stuck. I took a leap of faith to pursue a new career as an executive coach. This was the first lesson that William taught me and, as having kids so often does, it changed the trajectory of my life. For the first time, I was choosing my own path and embracing my own truth, as opposed to following the path I thought I was supposed to pursue.

Learning to "Be Yourself" in a Complicated World

At around the time William was seven, my wife, Susie, and I noticed that he was having issues with anxiety. He simply wanted to be himself and didn't know how. At times it got so bad that he developed a nervous tick. He would twitch his neck to one side, almost as if he was trying to stretch a tight muscle. It broke my heart every time I saw him twitch. I desperately wanted to help but didn't know how. At Susie's urging, we decided to send William to therapy — a fateful and positive decision. Through much hard work, he gradually became more at ease with himself and more self-assured. As tough as it was to see him struggle, it was truly amazing and beautiful to behold him turn a corner and begin to thrive. His hard work and persever-ance gave him the tools he would need to navigate life's many twists and turns. Witnessing someone grow and develop their own sense of self is a reminder of what this *one life* we have is all about: learning and evolving into our best possible selves, however that may unfold and however long we might live. We are each a work in progress — an imperfect lump of clay that gets molded into a meaningful shape by our life experiences.

As my own learnings started to take shape after William's death, poetry was the medium that spoke to me and allowed me to convey what arose from my inner being. As a teenager, I hated to write. I battled with my mother whenever she tried to coax me into writing a term paper for school. I refused to write the first drafts because the process of writing was so draining for me. But, as it turns out, a poem is very different from a term paper. I am, admittedly, not accustomed to leading with my emotions, so something about the brevity of a poem allowed my thoughts and feelings to come out on the page — quickly and without the angst I once experienced when writing longer essays or reports.

Often out of nowhere, a poem would come to me. Sometimes I would be in the shower or running an errand. The poems were always about William and our family — about life, loss, and love. Whenever they came, I would jot the poems down as quickly as I could in a notebook or on my iPhone. In the end, I am left with a collection of poems that has enabled me to convey the essence of the different experiences (and lessons) that surrounded William's death. These poems allowed me to write the following book chapters as they are now presented to you. And while *My Teacher, My Son* is my own personal story and a tribute to the life of an incredible little boy and his brothers, it is my hope that the poems — in all their intensity and perhaps universality — will resonate with you and allow you to connect with your own experiences of life, love, loss, change, opportunity, and transformation.

Witnessing someone grow and develop their own sense of self is a reminder of what this *one life* we have is all about: learning and evolving into our best possible selves, however that may unfold and however long we might live.

Just as William was coming into his own —learning to "be himself" — his life was cut short at nine years old. When he died, he was doing the thing he loved most (skiing) and was not just tackling literal mountain peaks but was at the metaphorical peak of who he was — a kind and old soul whose compassion and sensitivity for others drew people to him. When I picture William skiing on that last day of his life, the sun gleaming off his bright neon-orange helmet, he is at ease with himself as he lets gravity take over and trusts his body to flow with the terrain. He effortlessly glides in and out of each turn as if being led by the rhythmic beat of a spiritual drum that only he can hear. I continue to watch him as he gets farther and farther away from me, skiing off into the abyss of the world beyond. He isn't overthinking things or worried about outcomes. He has let go; he is happy. In that moment, he had achieved what so many strive for during much longer lives — the ability to be at peace with oneself.

My Teachers, My Sons

I will be the first to admit that if William had not died in 2019, I probably never would have written a book. So, while the title of this book is inspired by my eldest child's life and legacy, *My Teacher, My Son* is not only about William, but also about Kai and Bodhi. Kai and Bodhi are integral parts of the story, and both have taught me lessons of their own. This book is also about my wife, Susie, who you met in the Prologue and whose strength in those darkest moments held me up at a time where there seemed to be no other option but to fall. Lastly, the pages that follow are about the human spirit that amazingly shows up to bring light to the darkest of moments. I hope you feel that as you read and reflect — that you find yourself less alone with your own challenges and losses.

Writing this book has helped me process my grief, as well as to more deeply fulfill my purpose in life — "to learn so I can teach." It has also given me a way to keep William's spirit alive and to approximate the impact I know he would have had were his life not shortened. Lessons on how to live more fully and how to love more fully can emerge from our darkest hours. It's these lessons and my stories of learning that I want to share with you.

> **Writing this book has helped me process my grief, as well as to more deeply fulfill my purpose in life — "to learn so I can teach." It has also given me a way to keep William's spirit alive and to approximate the impact I know he would have had were his life not shortened.**

The Moments

The glow of a pre-dawn fire.
The stillness that is present
before the world awakens.
A hug — from not one ... not two ... but three
of the people you love most.
The excitement, after a year of waiting,
in finally making it to the mountain top.
A view so majestic that you appreciate
how Big the Sky really is.

A harrowing search
for one you love so.
The painful anticipation
of not knowing what will be.
The shock and pain
once the worst has been confirmed.
The numbness that takes over
as things will never be the same.
The moments,
big and small,
magnificent and tragic.

Noel

CHAPTER 1

FEBRUARY 19, 2019, began in the most beautiful of ways. We were on vacation in Big Sky, Montana. As is often the case in our family, I was the first one up, beginning my day around 6:00 a.m. As I looked out the frosted panes of the windows, the sun was just starting to rise. Crystals of powdery snow, blowing from the trees in a light wind, glistened in the morning light. I could tell that it had the makings of a beautiful day. We were staying in a charming log cabin at the foot of the slopes, and the cabin was completely quiet and calm that morning. The cabin offered the perfect setting for our family to enjoy each other's company. It had two bedrooms and one large rustic main room, the walls lined with exposed logs. The main room had an open floor plan. On one side, there was a small kitchen with all the essentials. On the other side was a seating area with couches and a coffee table, all framed by a wool rug with dark hues that tied together the room's aesthetic. In one corner, a cozy light brown leather chair and ottoman were clustered around a converted woodstove. There was a chill in the air, so I switched on the gas fireplace and, immediately, a flame sprung to life. The glow of the fire drew me over, and I took advantage of the stillness to settle into the chair and read a book. As a morning person and an introvert, I cherish these moments. It is that magical time of day — before life begins to emerge — where anything is possible. About a half-hour later, Susie got up and came to cuddle with me in the chair. Minutes later, William wandered into the living room and climbed on top us, followed by Kai. My peace and quiet was replaced with the warmest and most satisfying of family "pig piles," a truly special way to start the day.

Early morning, February 19, 2019, in Big Sky, Montana. Susie
extracts herself from the family "pig pile" in the leather chair
to photograph Nick with William (left) and Kai (right).

The plan for the day included the kids attending ski school in the morning.
This would give me a chance to ski alone, allowing me to push myself on
some of the more challenging slopes on the mountain. Susie would stay
home and get some much-needed quiet time before meeting the kids for
lunch after ski school. I would join them, then William and I would test our
mettle on Lone Peak, the highest part of the mountain. At just six years old,
Kai was already starting to become a good skier, but he wasn't quite ready to
take on Lone Peak. Instead, he and Susie would have their own adventure
skiing together for a couple hours on the lower part of the mountain. This
suited Susie just fine, as she enjoyed skiing at a more mellow and less
intense pace. After a few hours on our separate adventures, we would all
meet and ski as a family. It was a day's agenda of "ski, ski, and ski again."

I set out alone to try and catch the first lift of the day. As I had predicted, it was beautiful day. The air was crisp and the snow was just right — not too hard and icy and not too soft and slushy. I skied some easier runs at first to get warmed up and then, as I was about to get on a chairlift, I ran into our friends from our hometown of Carlisle, Massachusetts, the Svatek family: Matt and Jessie and their kids Eli (9) and Tori (6). We had flown out with them and the plan all along was to make the excursion to Lone Peak later that afternoon together. It was a nice surprise to get to ski with them that morning as well. We skied a couple runs together and then all headed down to the base of the mountain to meet up with Susie, William, and Kai. William was eager to get going. So instead of sitting for lunch, he and I grabbed some snacks and began the trek to Lone Peak. Getting to Lone Peak was an expedition itself. You had to take two different chair lifts, then make your way across to the base of Lone Peak where an aerial tram transported you up the steep and jagged face of the mountain. The tram could hold 15 skiers and, given the beautiful weather conditions that day, there was sure to be a crowd.

Nick, William, and Kai outside the cabin at mid-day
on February 19, 2019, in Big Sky, Montana.

Journey to the Top

We set off excited and full of energy, the kids eagerly pushing as fast as possible with their ski poles to get to our destination sooner. When we reached the tram, we were dismayed to see a line had formed and that we would have to wait nearly an hour to board. But our high spirits prevailed. We were determined to make it to the top and, with the sun shining bright up above, we were happy to wait it out. The kids were a bit restless and began to roughhouse. We quickly settled them down to avoid disturbing others in line by bribing them with some candy. They rejoiced in their treats, Eli feeding William Skittles through his balaclava, a head covering designed to protect your entire face from the cold. A humorous sight to behold.

Before we knew it, it was our turn to board the tram. William and I were able to make it to the front of the tram, which gave us a bird's eye view of the mountain as we made the steep climb to the top. The ascent was both spectacular and daunting. As the tram inched higher, we got a fresh sense of how big and steep the mountain really was. William was quiet and reflective, as he looked out the window at the challenge that lay ahead. This was often his way. He would turn inward to prepare himself and to quiet any anxious thoughts. Skiing the top of the mountain was a big deal for him. The year before, we had tried to ski Lone Peak, but we never made it there because we got stuck on a chair lift for two hours. It had been a huge disappointment for him, and this was his chance to finally make it to the top. The dream deferred was about to be the dream redeemed.

Skiing has always been a big part of my life. My father used to take me and my brother on ski trips when we were growing up. As a child, like William, I was initially short on confidence and full of anxiety. I am a fraternal twin and my brother always seemed to be a few steps ahead of me in whatever we did. Skiing was one of the few activities where the tables were turned and my confidence in my abilities was unwavering. When I was out on the mountain, all my worries disappeared. I didn't doubt myself and I was able to focus on the present moment. Skiing had become a passion for me, and, to this day, I find joy and my personal state of "flow" when the cold wind hits my face as I glide down the mountain. William competed on our local mountain's ski team in the neighboring town, and as he got older and stronger and gained more confidence, I could sense he felt the same way. A sense of comfort and exhilaration on the slopes was something we shared, something that bonded us in a very tight way. Getting up to Lone Peak was a big deal for me, too. As a father, sharing one of my passions with my son was something I had dreamed about since the day he was born. It wasn't an experience I wanted to force (surely, it was possible my children wouldn't have a passion or aptitude for skiing), but having that dream come to life was a very special gift.

A sense of comfort and exhilaration on the slopes was something we shared, something that bonded us in a very tight way. Getting up to Lone Peak was a big deal for me, too.

Blue Bird Day

Once you summit Lone Peak, the back of it opens into a bowl, carved by a wide expanse of ski runs. The conditions were perfect that day. In skiing terms, it's what you call a "Blue Bird Day," when the sun shines so brightly that the blueness of the sky pops in contrast to the whiteness of the snow. We got off the tram and, after taking a few pictures, we clicked into our ski bindings and got on our way. On our first run, William had the run of his life — skiing better than I had ever seen him ski before. He was magnificent. The run was not groomed, which meant that with each turn he made, his body was jolted by the bumps in the snow. Instead of resisting each blow, he absorbed it with his body and used the momentum to launch him into his next turn. It was as if he were dancing, letting the mountain be his lead as he continued down the slope. He made it look easy, and it's not. I followed him down the run with a GoPro video camera, attached to my chest, filming his every move. I was bursting at the seams with pride. He was fearless and confident as he made his way down. He had achieved that thrilling moment in every child skier's life: skiing the double black diamonds.[1] He was at the top of his game.

William Shaw (9) with Eli Svatek (9) and Tori Svatek (6) at the top of Lone Peak.

William and I skied with the Svateks for a couple more runs, but then — aware that the day was getting away from us — realized we needed to get to the bottom of the mountain to meet up with Susie and Kai. We said goodbye to the Svateks and began our trek back to the base of the mountain. On our way down, we took a wrong turn and found ourselves on a catwalk, a relatively flat road that winds its way down the mountain in switchbacks, providing an easier route to the bottom than a straight, steep run. Cut into the side of the mountain, the trail was flanked by steep, forested slopes, the base of the trees blanketed in deep powder snow. As was often the case on these runs, the momentum of my weight increased my speed, and carried me about 10 feet in front of William. I didn't think anything of it. I would periodically look back to make sure I didn't get too far ahead of William. On these catwalk runs, you literally just stand on your skis and glide — barely needing to make any turns, losing yourself in

---

[1] Double black diamond slopes are the most challenging runs on the mountain, designated for experts only.

the gentle, winding ride down the mountain. At one point, I even called Susie to let her know that we were five minutes away. The trail curved and a skier came whizzing past, "Was that your kid who went into the woods?" The words trailed behind him. He never stopped and zoomed right past me down the mountain, gone before I could fully process his question.

My mind jumped immediately to a picture of William catching an edge, veering off the run and getting stuck in the deep powder just off the trail. I stopped, popped off my skis, and headed back up the slope. When I rounded the curve in the slope, I found myself alone, the only sound being the crunching of the snow beneath my heavy ski boots. The stillness was eerie. I kept walking further up the slope, expecting to see William. I saw nothing. Normally when a skier strays off a groomed slope into powder snow, the tracks or an impression in the snow where they might have fallen or struggled can be seen. There were no signs in the snow. None. It was as if William had disappeared into thin air. I called out his name as loudly as I could. "William!!! William!!!" Silence. Between yells, I begged him to call back, *"Come on buddy, say something!"* I'm not sure if I whispered it or simply thought it. I was starting to worry.

I eventually went back to where my skis were and attempted to search for William in the trees, but the snow was so deep and heavy in the wooded area that I sunk down to my chest, trapped. I struggled to free myself and I had to use all my strength to claw my way out. A guest services attendant was skiing by and stopped when he saw my skis on the side of the slope and asked if I needed help. When I finally made it to him, exhausted and out of breath, I explained to him what had happened, and he radioed to ski patrol to come help. As I waited for them to arrive, I called Susie to let her know what had happened. Moments later, two or three ski patrollers, wearing bright red jackets, arrived and began to scan the area to determine where William might have gone off the side of the slope. I stationed myself where I had taken off my skis, not wanting to leave, but eventually the searchers suggested I ski to the bottom to see if William was there. They couldn't find any tracks in the woods and thought he may have somehow skied past me.

As I skied down to the bottom, I ran five words over and over in my head: "It's going to be fine; it's going to be fine; it's going to be fine." William must have kept going through the trees and made his way to the bottom. Anxiety and hope became my companions as I continued to the bottom, the two conflicting emotions battling each other for my attention.

I searched the lift lines, the lodge, the crowds of tired skiers preparing to take their last runs of the day. There were a few times when I thought I saw William's bright orange ski helmet or his curly blond hair. Each time I was crushed to find that it was another child. I fully understood the severity of the situation, but in my hopeful and panicked mind, there was no way that the worst could have possibly happened — not to William and not to our family.

Dusk

The sun was just starting to dip behind the mountain, blanketing the base in a shadow and causing the temperature to drop. I was suddenly aware of the chill and the implication of sunset giving way to darkness. The timing of the events is still quite murky in my memory, but I believe at that point William had been missing for perhaps an hour and a half. It must have been 3:30 or 4:00 p.m. and the thought of him being alone out there in the cold started to torment me.

A female ski patroller had joined me to help me search the base of the mountain. As we came out from the lodge, her walkie-talkie crackled alive with chatter. William had been found but was unresponsive. *Found but unresponsive.* The words struck my chest. My heart sank, and I dropped to my knees. The adrenaline rush that had kept me going during the search started to abate and I began to feel nauseated. Just at that point, I remember a random skier asking the ski patroller for directions. I remember thinking, in that moment, this person passing by had no idea of the tragedy that was unfolding—his innocent and commonplace question in the midst of my terror and pain was jarring.

Earlier, Susie had run into our friend Matt Svatek and his family on the mountain as she and Kai were making their way back to the cabin to see if William had somehow skied home. Matt was a firefighter with rescue experience, and he joined the search as soon as he got word. He was the one who found William. As William was being transported down the mountain, I was taken to the ski patrol clinic by a ski patroller on a snowmobile. The ride up the short hill from the base of the mountain to the clinic couldn't have been more than 300 yards. As we sped up the hill, the cold wind stung as it hit my face and my hands started to get numb. I remember feeling the cold but not caring. I just sat there on the snowmobile, holding on and staring in a zombie-like daze. I could barely comprehend what was happening.

Once at the clinic, I was ushered to a waiting room. The change in temperature was stifling. It was hot inside, but I didn't bother taking off my ski layers. The waiting room was sparsely furnished, so I just sat on the floor, leaning against the wall. A woman, who I believe was a nurse, sat next to me and tried to comfort me. But I was in a state of shock, and I was unable to process what she was saying. Everything was fuzzy.

I heard a helicopter landing outside. The sound instantly woke me and gave me a fleeting moment of hope that William was OK and would need to be air-lifted to a hospital in Bozeman for better treatment. Not too long after that, a wave of people burst into the clinic. I didn't see them but heard the commotion. William arrived and was immediately brought into a treatment room. I waited for a bit longer, still sitting on the floor, nervously rubbing my hands together. The lead doctor finally came out. As he approached, I still had some hope that things would be fine. Then I heard the words, "I am so sorry."

•   •   •

When I heard those words come out of the doctor's mouth, there was a momentary pause. The pause was infinitesimally brief, yet its magnitude was utterly immense. It created a dividing line between the life that once was and the uncertain life that would be. Right there, in that instant, my world was changed forever. My son had been a nine-year-old, skiing the best run of his life just hours before. And now ... he was gone. Even the doctor couldn't bring himself to say it. My son was dead.

The first stanza of the poem that begins this chapter describes how the day started on February 19, 2019, and the second stanza how the day ended. The momentary pause (perhaps with a small breath) you take as you end verse one and let your eyes transition to begin reading verse two is about how long it took for my world to be turned upside down. Until William's accident, life made sense. Then, in a matter of seconds, my expectations for how life would and should unfold were shattered. A life that seemed so secure and stable at the beginning of the day was lying in pieces all around me. I felt overwhelmed by uncertainty and a complete loss of control.

As I was forced to absorb this new reality, a deeper emotional shock began to flood my entire being, putting me into a state of suspended animation. I could feel myself starting to shut down as the trauma of everything took over. I barely felt human. As bad as it was at the time, I now realize that this forced and momentary pause was necessary for my survival. It was my body's way of protecting me. This idea of pausing is not something that came naturally to me, but it would prove to be a necessity that would allow me and my family to heal.

Ever since I was a boy, I always felt that I was playing catch-up. From about the age of seven, my fraternal twin brother, Claude, began to pull ahead of me in school as well as athletics. You can imagine that in my seven-year-old mind, none of this made sense. We were twins — equals. This wasn't supposed to be the way things were. As if that didn't create enough anxiety, I also found myself trying to live up to a father who, in my young mind, was an infallible "superman" for whom success was a birth right. The thing about always feeling like you must catch up is that pausing is not an acceptable option. If you do, you only fall further behind. Thus, my approach to life was always about moving forward and looking ahead. It was about always judging where I was vis-à-vis others, never really being quite at ease or present in any given moment. I was in a rush to achieve, succeed, and be enough. And then, the frenetic pace of my life changed instantly. There was nowhere to rush to. I was suspended in this moment of time.

The Paradox of Time

When you lose someone, especially when you lose a child, all you can think is, "If I only had more time." You long for so many things that could have been. I longed for more ski trips and seeing William grow up to become a man. Time, our scarcest of resources, becomes a measuring stick, as you question whether you had maximized the moments you had with them. *"Did I do enough? Did I love deeply enough? Was I truly present?"* Many of us live lives that are governed by busyness. Our focus tends to be more about where we are trying to get to as opposed to where we are in the present moment. My own life before the accident took on that pattern, which meant moments were about getting "from here to there" as efficiently as possible — constantly juggling the many different priorities in my life. I was still that seven-year-old kid playing catch up, forever chasing a finish line that always seemed to get farther and farther away. It's a feeling that had tormented me for much of my life. It was exhausting.

> ## When you lose someone, especially when you lose a child, all you can think is, "If I only had more time."

Ironically, at the end of 2018 (several months before our trip to Big Sky), I had an inkling that something was amiss. After having had my best year-to-date as a partner at the Exetor Group, a leadership development firm, I came to the realization that after having worked really hard, I would only be afforded a brief moment to celebrate and recharge before the clock would start all over again. A new year would mean pushing to exceed my performance from the prior year while much of my time (up to 50%) would be on the road and away from my family. This meant fifty percent fewer opportunities to spend time with William, who in a little over two months into the new year would be gone.

Throughout life, we experience a wide range of consequential moments — a series of highs and lows that stitch together our lives. On February 19, 2019, my family experienced the highest of highs and the lowest of lows.

The juxtaposition is staggering — as a day that started so magnificently ended so tragically. It shines a light on just how fragile life really is and that things can change in the blink of an eye. So, what does this mean, I wondered as I worked my way through my grief those first few weeks and months, for how we could live our lives differently once we acknowledge that fragility? Many of us are constantly in a state of distraction and a pull toward constant activity. I, for one, rarely stood still. Everyone is vying for our attention, it seems, and unfortunately, we give that time and attention away, all too easily, to things that are less meaningful to us. We worry incessantly about the small stuff, and all too often take our eyes off what is truly important. Or we convince ourselves that we can multi-task, never being fully present in any given moment. I'll be the first one to admit that I am guilty of this. So, if we are only half present in any given moment, would we consider it only half a moment? And if that were the case, would our lives only be half as meaningful? In the grand scheme of things, we are all here but for a precious and brief moment, which makes how we choose to live our lives more important.

> **On February 19, 2019, my family experienced the highest of highs and the lowest of lows. The juxtaposition is staggering — as a day that started so magnificently ended so tragically.**

My approach to living my life by constantly trying to win the battle over time wasn't working. Cramming as much as I could into this most limited of resources wasn't expanding it but rather compressing it. When we lost William, Susie and I gained a lot of time that passed in an excruciatingly slow manner. Life was no longer about swift days but painful minutes and hours. Doing more with less wasn't an option. I had no energy to fill the space. I needed to learn to do less with more. This is the paradox of time — instead of conquering time by rushing to fill every available moment, I needed to slow down and embrace it.

I chose to sit quietly in those slow-moving moments rather than rush through them, as I might once have done. I pressed pause on my career.

After William died, I took a six-month leave of absence from work to be with Susie and Kai and to try to make sense of everything. This pause gave me the time and space to reflect and ask, "Is this the way I want to go on living my life?" While the answer is important, I found that taking the time to ask the question is more important. If I hadn't asked the question, there is a high likelihood that I would have been stuck on autopilot and the opportunity to live in a more purposeful and deliberate way would have passed me by. When I am in this autopilot state, I lose sight of what's going on in the present moment because I worry too much about what *could* have been (the past) or what *might* be (the future). When I am present, I focus my attention on whatever a particular moment has in store for me. Whether a moment is magnificent or tragic, big or small, the more I attend to it, the more I can experience it with all my being. It could be as simple as taking in a majestic view or paying attention to the people I'm interacting with. I untether myself from my smart phone so I can legitimately be in the "here and now." I can connect with others in a more in-depth way and truly see them for who they are.

> **When I am present, I focus my attention on whatever a particular moment has in store for me. Whether a moment is magnificent or tragic, big or small, the more I attend to it, the more I can experience it with all my being.**

I know that I will never be fully free of the distractions of life, as some of those are necessary and important and because modern life in the 2020s leaves us with everyone and everything demanding our focus. Despite the challenges, I can be more intentional about the choices I make — about which moments are truly necessary and important and need my full attention (and which aren't). To do this "slowing down and pausing" is critical. It allows me to be more intentional about how I am showing up. I can silently ask myself, "Is this where my attention should be?" Should it be on that email notification that just dinged on my phone, or should it be on the opportunity to engage with my child? In the immediate aftermath of William's death, there was so much that demanded my focused attention. Susie needed me. Kai needed me. I needed to care for my own broken heart. Time slowed down and my vision narrowed.

As I wrote the first draft of this book's manuscript, I realized that pausing doesn't only have to occur in the big moments in life — the magnificent and the tragic. I wondered: Why not pause more frequently during the small moments? When I do this more often, I can get off the proverbial "hamster wheel" and can just be. I can be in the moment for whatever that moment has to offer. I can allow myself to be fully captivated and more at choice with who I would like to be and what impact I aspire to have. This is how I was able to make meaning out of the most tragic of events. My journey to find meaning in all of life's different moments continues. I just have to remember (and accept) that it is OK to pause every so often — for a minute or an hour, for a day, a week, or even six months.

Four Words

How could I look her in the eye?
He was with me when it happened.
One minute, he was there ...
and the next, he wasn't.

How could I look her in the eye?
Would this be the destruction
of three more lives?
Would we become just another statistic?

How could I look her in the eye?
What would she think of me,
he who lost this most precious gift?

When I finally looked her in the eye,
she said four words
that have allowed us to endure:
"It's not your fault."

CHAPTER 2

MY MIND WAS spinning, trying to rationally comprehend what
had just happened. The outside world, the clinic, the doctor, the over-
heated room — it all spun away from me, and I withdrew inward. I could
feel my temples pulsating and my brain was working hard to make sense
of it all. It hurt … not in an emotional way, but in a physical way. My head
throbbed. As I struggled to break from this trance, something rose like
a tidal wave from the depths of my subconscious. I was not alone in this
ordeal. The dam of rationality that had been holding back any emotional
outburst ruptured as I yelled, "What the fuck am I going to tell Kai?"

I slammed my hand against the wall. I had just lost my nine-year-old son
and now I had to give the devastating news to his six-year-old brother. It
was too much to take and I broke down. Matt was there, beside me. He
grabbed hold of me and gave me a big hug. Nothing in the world at that
moment could console me because I had to tell Susie and Kai that William
died. But how? The thought of facing them scared me to death. William
was with *me* when the accident happened and the one and only thought
that took over was that "this was my fault."

Susie and I had been in a steady flow of communication as the search for
William was unfolding. She had gone back to our cabin with Jessie Svatek,
hoping to find William there. In the last call I made to her, I told her that
things were bad and that she had to get to the clinic as soon as possible.
I didn't want to tell her over the phone that William had died. She needed
to hear it from me in person. As I waited for her, my head continued to
spin. I was scared. I was scared to devastate her with this horrible news.
I was scared for what this would do to our family. Would we become
three more victims — a couple divorced and a surviving child who was

so scarred by what happened that he never recovered? These thoughts churned in my head over and over as guilt consumed my mind and body. I paced back and forth manically as I waited for her. How was I going to tell her? What words does one use when something like this happens?

And then she was there. Susie's eyes met mine across the room. Standing about 10 feet apart, I told her that William had died. There was a split-second pause, when time seemed to be momentarily trapped in the uncertainty of everything. Then as if in slow motion, Susie crumbled to the floor. My instincts quickly took over and I ran over to her. As I pulled her up to me, she looked me deeply in the eyes, put both hands on my shoulders and said, "It's not your fault." Her response stunned me. Then, I felt an overwhelming sense of relief. It was one of those fork-in-the-road moments. It would have been understandable if she had a different reaction, but she chose that one. Instead of blaming me, she absolved me. Her choice of words and attitude in that moment set the tone for how our family would endure the challenging road that lay ahead, and I am forever grateful to her for that. She was the embodiment of selflessness, putting aside her pain momentarily to take care of me and our family.

· · ·

To this day, I am in awe of how Susie showed up in our darkest of moments. What happened to our family that day was unimaginable and completely beyond our control. Susie's actions that day epitomize the notion that in any moment — even the most shattering — we can choose how we react.

I did a lot of reading in the months after William's death. One of the books that left a particularly strong impression on me was *Man's Search for Meaning* by Viktor Frankl. Viktor Frankl was a Holocaust survivor, and in his book, he describes the horrifying ordeal and how he was able to survive:

> "Everything can be taken from a man but one thing: the last of the human freedoms — to choose one's attitude in any given set of circumstances, to choose one's own way."

It was this key element that enabled Frankl to endure the physical and psychological torment that his Nazi captors were imposing on him. When literally everything was stripped away from him, the one thing his captors couldn't take was his power to choose how he reacted. Ultimately, it is one of the only things that is unequivocally within our control. And Susie's actions that day — when she chose to love me, instead of blame me — are a testament to this truth.

The Deepest, Darkest Valley

I am old enough now to realize that life is going to surprise us and that the journey is always a blend of different experiences — some good, and some bad. And we don't know what's coming, or when. I've come to think of life as a series of peaks and valleys, and often just when we feel like things couldn't be better, a curve ball knocks us off that peak and we find ourselves down in the deepest, darkest valley. Then what? It's here — in those moments of darkness — that our reactions and attitudes determine what our "valley" experience will be like and whether, how, and how soon we will work our way out of it. The choices we make can have a huge impact on ourselves and the people around us.

I sometimes wonder what would have happened if Susie had had a different reaction to the news of our son's death. What if, instead of forgiving me, she had blamed me for what happened? It would have been an understandable reaction. Of course, we were both thinking, "How could this have happened?!" and it would have been entirely natural for Susie to say (or even scream) it out loud in a way that was accusatory. Had she done that, it would have set into motion an entirely different course for how things may have unfolded for our family. In that moment — those initial seconds that are now frozen in our memories — I was so tormented by an all-consuming guilt that an angry, blameful reaction from my wife may have pushed me over the edge. Who knows what I might have done? It's only human for our emotions to get the best of us in extreme situations, and for us to do or say something that we might regret later. I will spend the rest of my life feeling grateful that, imperfect as we were in the early moments of our grief, neither Susie nor I walked away regretful for our own reactions.

In the coming days, weeks, and months after William's death, I confronted what had been a lifetime of limiting beliefs. Feelings from my own childhood and my early professional career reared their ugly heads and compounded my grief. Without meaning to, I fell back into old patterns of self-doubt and self-blame. For me, the narrative that formed when I was seven was that I was "the lesser twin." When I was growing up, this internal story served to provide me with a clear sense of where I was in the pecking order, and it kept me in my place. This "second place" attitude had become so ingrained in me that no matter how destructive and limiting this belief has been, it provided me with comfort — in childhood and even in my adulthood.

In my processing of what happened to William, there were countless times where I allowed this old "I am less than" narrative to convince me that what had happened to William was just another part of that story — the story that said I wasn't allowed to have it all: the successful career, the beautiful family. It all seemed to fit together so conveniently, and it did nothing to alleviate the pain I was going through. It only made it worse. In resigning myself to the deepest, darkest part of the emotional valley — as if this kind of loss was my destiny — I allowed our circumstances to take away my power and make me into a victim. The choice, I initially thought, was made for me from deep within — that past was prologue and that my history of being the underdog was now playing out in a particularly cruel and painful way. In feeling that "of course horrible things would happen to me," I was relinquishing the one thing that I truly had control over — my mindset. I have had many such moments since February 2019, where I could go deeper into my grief or somehow pull myself up above it. And sometimes when I catch myself going darker and deeper, I use Susie as my inspiration. I think of her reaction on that fateful day — of those four words ("It's not your fault.") — and I am reminded that I have the power to choose.

The choice, I initially thought, was made
for me from deep within — that past was
prologue and that my history of being
the underdog was now playing out in
a particularly cruel and painful way. In
feeling that "of course horrible things
would happen to me," I was relinquishing
the one thing that I truly had control over
— my mindset.

We all do. We must remember that when we're at the mercy of uncontrollable circumstances, we can wrestle control back by choosing our reaction
— in finding the courage to make a different choice from the default
option to blame or wallow or worse. This is the lesson that Susie taught me
that day. That I can always choose love (and self-love), forgiveness (and
self-forgiveness), and the resolution to keep going.

To Be Seen by a Stranger

As I stand here before you
and you pull me in tight,
my tears become your tears.

As you hold me there longer,
I have not one ounce of doubt
that this feeling so deep unites us.

You don't even know me.
And yet, in this moment,
we are the two most connected people on Earth.

CHAPTER 3

SUSIE AND I broke from our embrace. The time had come for us
to see William. Until this point, the thought of William's death was just
that — a thought. We had been told that William had died but we had not
fully experienced it. Now was the moment we were forced to face it. As
we were ushered into the room where William had been treated, I kept
thinking, "We are those people." We are those people from countless TV
scenes and movie moments — those people who must now see their child
lying motionless and cold on a table. It's every parent's nightmare. Even
as we were walking into that room, it all seemed so surreal. As my shock
gave way to denial, I felt as if I was having an out-of-body experience and
I was watching the scene unfold from afar. I felt bad for the people in the
scene, and in that brief moment there was a sense of separation between
me and them.

Until there wasn't.

The room was small, and the table William was lying on took up most of
the space. Even if we had wanted to look away, it was impossible. William
was the focal point of the room as he lay there on the table. He didn't look
blue or stiff, and had it not been for the intubation tube in his mouth,
you might have thought he was simply sleeping. He looked peaceful and
calm — like most children do when they're asleep. We stood there in the
doorway in silence. Both Susie and I struggled to make sense of what we
were seeing. Our brains were hopelessly trying to come up with answers.
Part of us hoped he would wake up and part of us knew it would never be.
It was too much for us to handle and both Susie and I stepped toward the
table and flung ourselves over William, trying to give him every ounce of
love that we had in our bodies. We wanted to hug and hold him as tightly
as we could and never let go. As we did, our pain only magnified in our
visceral shrieks and cries. It was gut wrenching.

We were so engrossed in William that we didn't initially notice the EMT who accompanied us into the room. This was part of the protocol, and his job was to stand in the room with us to make sure we wouldn't become a risk to ourselves or anyone else. I finally stepped away from William and, as I straightened up, I noticed the EMT standing in front of me. Our eyes met and through my own tears, I could see that he was also crying. The weight of the moment — like a magnet — pulled us closer, and he gave me big hug. We stood there for a couple of minutes crying in each other's arms. As we did, I could sense that he was feeling what I was feeling. It's as if, when we hugged, our emotions had become fused. He was with me in that moment. I was no longer alone with my emotion. The grief that Susie and I were experiencing was already bigger than the two of us. As the EMT and I broke from our hug, we looked each other in the eye one last time and, without saying a word, we both knew that we were bonded by that moment. Several weeks later, I reached out to him to thank him for what he had done. I don't know how well I conveyed to him the impact he had on me, but it will forever be one of the most beautiful acts of humanity that I have ever experienced. On that day, he connected with my deepest and rawest emotions.

•　　•　　•

As human beings, we all want to be seen. We want to be acknowledged and understood, no matter how we show up. The key to this is empathy — the ability to put yourself in someone else's shoes and feel what they might be feeling. And the result is connecting with them in a deeper way. In my work as an executive coach, I often talk about empathy as an important leadership skill, but it wasn't until that moment with the EMT that I truly experienced it. I don't typically lead with my emotions; I tend to be more reserved and guarded. My way of processing is using my head to think things through as opposed to using my heart to feel into a situation. Perhaps that's why I had never fully experienced or appreciated true empathy up until then. Having always been somewhat guarded, it was perhaps hard for others to connect with me emotionally, because the emotion — from my side of the equation — was not as apparent. But the raw nature of my emotion after seeing William on that table was too much for me to contain and overpowered my tendency to be guarded. My walls came crumbling down. I was exposed and vulnerable and broken.

**I don't typically lead with my emotions;
I tend to be more reserved and guarded.
My way of processing is using my head
to think things through as opposed to
using my heart to feel into a situation.**

The EMT met me where I was. He, too, let himself be exposed and vulnerable and we had a profound moment of connection. His hug and his tears were a gift to us in our darkest moment.

There Are No Words

I have always struggled with knowing how to be overtly empathetic. I am never quite sure what to say in emotional moments, and when I do say something, it feels awkward. It's not that I'm heartless or unaware — I pick up on the emotion that is present and can put myself in the other person's shoes. But whether people know that I'm empathetic is a different matter, because I am less assured in how best to respond. I get more concerned with my own awkwardness than I am with what is going on with the other person. I care, but don't always know how to show it.

In the end, I am afraid to open myself up for fear of being judged and coming across as weak. It's how I was brought up and what was modeled for me as a boy. My parents couldn't have been at more opposite ends of the emotional spectrum. My mother, who was born in Argentina, was a walking emotion. We always knew how she was feeling. My father, on the other hand, was much more guarded and rarely — if ever — had any big emotional reactions. Naturally, I gravitated in that direction because, as a boy, that's how I thought men were supposed to be. I learned to keep my emotions close to the vest, as they say.

The experience with the EMT taught me the power of emotional connection. And I immediately understood the value of such connection. I now realize that to benefit from connection, I must be less guarded. For an empathetic response to be genuine, I must be vulnerable — willing to express the emotion I am feeling. The EMT didn't lose his child that day, but I can assure you that he felt the sadness and grief that Susie and I were feeling. He allowed himself to experience those raw emotions and then expressed them. True empathy is a selfless act. We don't worry about what people will think if we give a stranger a hug or if we burst into tears in public. We open ourselves emotionally for the sake of another. We put our "selves" aside so that we can connect with and support someone who needs us.

William didn't do what I did as a child — he didn't become stoic because he saw his father modeling stoicism. He was a naturally empathetic and compassionate person. He genuinely cared for others and was always sensitive to what another person needed. I can remember countless times when I would get frustrated about this or that and William would just look at me with understanding eyes, giving me the space I needed. Any time a new child joined the class at school, they were seated next to William. When a Syrian refugee family moved to our town, William was chosen to help the child in his grade assimilate. This is what William was all about — and the day we lost him, we lost a truly compassionate soul.

We need more Williams in this world — more compassionate souls, more people who can be counted on to befriend the new kid. We need more people to remember that we are more than just the labels or roles that are ascribed to us. We are human. We are all just trying to figure out how to live our lives amidst all the chaos. In some ways, the moment we lost William's compassionate humanity, we saw it incarnate in another — in the EMT who showed me the true power of the human spirit.

We need more Williams in this world — more compassionate souls, more people who can be counted on to befriend the new kid.

Indeed, that hug from a stranger was but a small moment, lasting just a few poignant minutes, but it impacted me deeply and has left an impression on me that I will never forget. What if this was the kind of impact we could have on each other more often and not just in times of tragedy? Perhaps this world we live in would be ever so slightly less chaotic and cold.

What if this was the kind of impact we could have on each other more often and not just in times of tragedy? Perhaps this world we live in would be ever so slightly less chaotic and cold.

The Missing Seat

No longer separated by an aisle,
we seem to fit so perfectly.

To the unwitting passerby,
it would seem to be so.

But to a heart so broken,
nothing could be further from the truth.

CHAPTER 4

AFTER SPENDING A bit more time with William at the clinic, Susie and I realized that we needed to go and get Kai, who was with the Svatek kids and their grandmother at their vacation condo. Matt and Jesse escorted us out of the clinic and drove us to their condo. As we sat in the car in silence on the short drive to their place, nothing seemed real. I felt like I was in a perpetual dream state. I was exhausted. I was in shock. And despite it all, I was going to need to compose myself so I could deliver the terrible news to Kai.

When we walked into the Svateks' condo, we found the kids playing board games. They were so innocent, not knowing the full extent of the tragedy that had unfolded that day and, therefore, not knowing to be worried, scared, or sad just yet. They looked happy. They were having fun. I watched Kai for a minute, and realized what I was about to do; I was going to take that innocence and expose it to one of life's harshest realities. I didn't want to do it but there was no other option. Susie and I went over to Kai and asked him to come with us into one of the bedrooms. I sat him on my lap and said, "There was an accident. Your brother won't be coming back. He is in heaven." It's all I could come up with.

Saying those 14 words to our youngest son was probably the most difficult thing I have ever had to do. Kai just sat on my lap, not knowing how to react. He didn't cry and he didn't say anything; he just looked at me. It was too much for his 6-year-old brain to comprehend and he eventually got down and went back to the other room to continue playing. I realized then that it would take time for him to understand everything — that as he got older and continued to mature, he would continue to process this in his own way. We spent a bit more time at the Svateks' condo and then headed back to our cabin.

Kai at age six, February 2019

When we eventually made it back to the cabin, the cozy den that had been our source of warmth and comfort became our own personal hell. The shock of the day hit particularly hard after we put Kai to bed. No longer needing to put on a brave face for him, I found myself on the floor in front of the fireplace in the fetal position shaking uncontrollably. The log-lined walls of the cabin — which had once seemed so charming — now felt as if they were closing in on us. The comforting glow of the fire — which had warmed our hearts that morning and the previous night — now took on a more ominous hue, as I contemplated whether I could go on. In that moment, it seemed like the best answer was to end it all and join William. I was lost and I was broken.

Susie sensed that she had to take control, and she did. She suggested that the best thing for us was to leave Montana as soon as possible. William's body was going to be taken to the coroner in Bozeman and then would be flown to Massachusetts once arrangements had been made for his funeral. There was no reason to stay in Montana and endure the hell we were experiencing. Susie relentlessly scrolled through travel options on her phone to get us home as soon as possible and she was able to get us on a flight the next day. With that task behind her, she single-handedly packed everything up and got us ready to make the long trek home to Massachusetts. Susie's strength that night was superhuman. I can only imagine how deep she had to dig, amidst her own trauma and grief, to muster up the energy to complete this colossal task. I watched in a daze as she handled the logistics during the worst night of our lives.

The next day, we boarded a flight from Bozeman to Denver and then another flight from Denver to Boston. Susie and I were still in a state of shock as we began to feel the full force of our grief. It's an odd state to be in. Tragedy suspended us in a constant state of flux between the surreal and the real. In the surreal moments, we floated along in a bad dream, comforted by the thought that at any moment we might wake up and things would be back to normal. I kept observing myself and what was happening (to me and around me) from afar — with a sense of detach- ment as if I was watching a movie. Then, out of nowhere, some small reminder would jolt me awake. I would break out of my dream only to find myself in a nightmare, and the one thing I longed for was to return to that numbed, surreal state. Now — fully awake — the reality of it was the only thing I could focus on. Over and over, the reality of William's death would hit me so suddenly and acutely that my emotional pain became physical. It's like being doused with freezing cold water. The shock literally stopped me in my tracks. For me, it hit right in my chest — hard enough to make me wince and recoil as I clutched at my heart.

The shock hit me first on that plane ride home when we made our way up the center aisle of the first plane. With three seats on either side, we had always spread our family of four across the aisle — accustomed to dividing our family by seating a parent and two kids on one side and the other parent across the aisle. This flight was tragically different as the three of us took our seats on only one side of the aisle. For the past six years, since Kai was born, we'd been a family of four; this wasn't right. I sat between Susie and Kai, so that I could take care of Kai and give Susie a break. She had expended every bit of energy the night before, trying to get us home.

The flight from Bozeman to Denver was a little over an hour, but it seemed to last an eternity. We were physically trapped by the confines of the plane and mentally trapped by the constant reminder of how things used to be. There was no escaping this hellish reality. Fortunately, on the last and longer leg of the trip, we found moments of distraction by watching movies on the plane's entertainment system. I ended up watching *Bohemian Rhapsody* and, for at least two hours, was able to lose myself in someone else's story.

> ## The flight from Bozeman to Denver was a little over an hour, but it seemed to last an eternity. We were physically trapped by the confines of the plane and mentally trapped by the constant reminder of how things used to be.

Home, Quiet Home

We finally made it home, which provided some level of comfort. But everywhere we turned, the reminders of William were constant and relentless. The first thing Susie and I did when we walked into our house was to go to William's room. The bottom bunk of his green metal-framed bunk bed was still undone. The comforter and sheets were in a pile at the foot of the bed. Just five days earlier, he had sprung up out of bed at 3:30 a.m. — full of excitement and eagerness to make the trip to Montana. It looked now just as it did then — a moment frozen in time.

I had walked through that bedroom door thousands of times before and William's warmth was always there to greet me. I would play a little game with him where I would open his door, poke my head in, ask if he was ok, and then shut the door as if I were leaving. I would then repeat this — three or four more times — just to get a laugh out of him. Now, I didn't want to ever close that door.

The built-in bookshelves, which faced the door, were filled with his things just where he'd left them. His Legos were prominently displayed: castles, vehicles, Star Wars sets. Each creation was a reminder of the countless hours he and I spent building them — initially with me doing most of the work and eventually with him as the true expert builder and with me relegated to just watching him (and occasionally being asked to find a Lego piece that he needed). I could sit there for hours just watching him build. Now, on February 20th, I could see him without even closing my eyes. He was here in this room, and yet he wasn't.

On the rest of his shelves were the knick-knacks that he had picked up on different family trips we had taken together, like his camouflage Swiss Army knife and the ceramic Día de Los Muertos skull that was a souvenir from a trip to Mexico. Neatly arranged on the shelves, these treasures formed a rainbow of different colors.

William's ski-racing ribbons hung off one of the bed posts. The ribbons told the story of his progress — from 8th place to 6th place to 5th place to 4th place and finally to 3rd place. Everything was just where it should have been, yet the one thing that really gave the room life was missing. He was missing. The weight of reality was too much, and Susie and I broke down and cried in each other's arms.

Without William, his room was too lifeless and empty; it was no longer a place where we felt comforted or comfortable. We realized we needed to change that. We didn't want William's space to be abandoned and untouchable, like an old museum exhibit trapped in time and which occasionally people came to see, then never visit again. We wanted William's room to be a place where people could find comfort and solace — a place where they could connect with William. So, after some deliberation, we decided to redo his room.

About a month or so after getting home, we replaced his bunk bed with a daybed covered in plush pillows and blankets, an inviting space to get cozy. We papered the entire wall facing the daybed with a mural depicting a forest scene with rays of orange and yellow sunshine emerging through large oak trees. The moment you walk into the redecorated room, the landscape and colors transport you outdoors to the middle of nature, a place where William loved to be. On the wall behind the day bed is now a sign for the trail where William died. It had been renamed Skittles Road two years later in memory of William by the company who owns and operates Big Sky.

We had a built-in window bench installed, which created another seating area for lounging. We wanted to create a room with enough space for us to comfortably be together as a family but that was not overcrowded with furniture. For me, the revitalized but sacred space was where I spent the first moments of every day for the next six months; I came to meditate, trying to make sense out of everything that had happened.

In William's remodeled room.

William's room wasn't the only part of the house that got a "makeover" — every inch of the house seemed different, even if it wasn't. One of the most notable and inescapable changes to our new reality — minute to minute and hour to hour — was how quiet our house had become. With two boys, just two and half years apart, our house had always been flooded with their voices and sounds and noises. Whether it was laughter as they played together or their bickering as they pestered each other, the soundtrack of William and Kai was always present in our home.

Anyone who has children or grew up with siblings knows how much bickering becomes a part of life. There were so many times when it drove me crazy to the point of losing my temper and having to use my "dad voice," yelling at them to stop. "Boys! Enough! Please stop." Now, I would give anything to hear the sweet sounds of William and Kai arguing over the littlest things. Our house — once reverberating with the sounds of its four inhabitants — was now dominated by a deafening silence. Without someone for Kai to play and quarrel with, our house had become unbearably quiet.

> **Our house — once reverberating with the sounds of its four inhabitants — was now dominated by a deafening silence. Without someone for Kai to play and quarrel with, our house had become unbearably quiet.**

In those early days after William's death, we knew just two things. Our lives were forever changed, and we needed desperately to figure out how to move forward.

• • •

I don't think I had ever realized — until I became a bereaved parent — that our human resistance to change of any kind makes grief that much more difficult. There's not just the pain and despair, but also the persistent sense of being unsettled by change; and death is the greatest change of all. As an executive coach, I've spent a lot of time helping people process and work through change. There's an entire business discipline called "change management" because managing (and accepting) change is so difficult for nearly everyone. How was I supposed to "manage" this change?

Change is never easy — no matter what the situation. Most of us like the predictability of our routines and norms. They provide us with comfort as we grapple with the complexity and turmoil that surrounds us. When unwanted or unexpected change occurs, we resist it, clinging to what was. We fight it with the hopes of preserving the status quo or protecting our previous place of comfort. When William died, there was nothing we could do but confront the stark changes head on. There are no instructions for what to do when you lose a child. As someone who likes a clearly defined path, this was very difficult for me. I wanted to know the "right" path to allowing our family to heal. Everywhere I turned, things looked unfamiliar. And as I strove to find answers to bring about some sense of certainty, I only found more questions.

One question I grappled with was what I should do with respect to my work. Should I go back right away or take time off? And, if I took time off, how much time? My life had always been centered around trying to control outcomes with structure and routine. It was about staying active and moving forward. Not going back to work meant my days would lack the structure that work provided; this would only bring more ambiguity to my already unraveled life. I was afraid of losing another part of myself. In the end, I had no choice but to take a six-month leave of absence from my place of employment, as I realized that I would be of no use to my clients or my colleagues in my current state. I pressed "pause" on my old life.

Like Sand Through an Hourglass

Initially, without the structure and routine to which I was so accustomed, the days seemed to last an eternity, one blending into the next. Time had become timeless. The comfort I had gotten from being overly scheduled was now gone. Other than helping Susie take care of Kai and other household chores, I spent a lot of time on the couch in my office. People would come to visit but my preference was to be alone. Kai went back to school several weeks after we returned home, and the house became even quieter. It felt like I was floating aimlessly in the dark abyss of space, with only my grief to keep me company. I tried in vain to force a structure to my days but was too apathetic and exhausted from grief to stick to any kind of routine. There was no rhyme or reason to anything. Being at home felt like being in prison and I questioned whether I had made the right decision regarding my leave of absence.

Initially, without the structure and routine to which I was so accustomed, the days seemed to last an eternity, one blending into the next. Time had become timeless.

Eventually, Susie and I both started to feel the strain of our grief and we decided to travel and visit friends. It was our way of escaping the constant reminders at home of what we had lost. It was also a way for us to focus our energies on bringing some joy, levity, adventure, and welcome new memories into Kai's life.

It wasn't until we were visiting our friends Laine and Scott in Thousand Oaks, California, that I realized that I had made the right decision regarding my leave. One night after dinner, I was having a conversation with Laine, and she helped me realize that the change we were wrestling with was how to become a family of three. It was not something that had been clear to me until Laine made that observation. Our focus, up until that moment, was primarily on the loss of William. Before William died, we were a family of four. There was a symmetry to it that worked — a cadence and rhythm to which we had become accustomed. We went from raising two kids who were able to entertain each other to suddenly raising an "only child" who had never known life without his older brother — always there to play with, talk to, and be with.

We needed this time together to learn how to be a family of three. Taking time off allowed me to actively participate in figuring things out together with Susie and Kai. Had I gone back to work prematurely, this process would have been delayed or may have unfolded very differently. Taking time off and visiting friends — as a family of three — helped us to recon-figure ourselves. Most importantly, it signaled to Kai that we were all in this together and that we would be OK.

Time kept passing. The change we were facing was so much more than "change" — it was doubly intertwined with our grief. We were not only grieving the loss of William but also the loss of how our family used to be. In some ways, it feels strange or even diminishing to talk about a death as a "change," but seeing it that way has helped me understand all the nuances of difficulty that I contended with after William's death. Surely, the loss of a loved one is perhaps one of the biggest and most impactful changes that can occur in one's life, but unwanted, unplanned change of any type or magnitude inevitably has some component of grief to it. We grieve what once was and is no longer. Change — by its very nature — brings about ambiguity and uncertainty. A core reason for resisting change is that, often, we are not clear about the change we are facing. We can't embrace or accept what we don't understand, so we resist. We know with certainty what we have lost (whether it's a loved one, a job, a relationship, a home, or a sense of security), but we can't always sense the scope and breadth of its impact on us.

For us, the "practical" change after William's death was the adjustment to living as (and seeing ourselves as) a family of three. It was hard and we resisted it, again and again. The broader lesson — for us and perhaps for the readers of this book — is when we start to understand how a change (any change, big or small!) affects us, we can begin the process of acceptance and moving forward. Without this understanding, it is very hard to figure out how to work through it. We can fight the new reality all we want (and we will — think about how we automatically start shouting or mumbling "no, no, no, no, no!" when facing a shocking new reality), but all that this fighting will do is delay the inevitable and will make the process more difficult and painful. Once we move past our initial shock, chronic resistance can't and won't serve us.

As I reflect on my own experiences with resistance and change — particularly my experiences as a grieving father — there are two key lessons I take away. The first is that it's important to always ask myself, "What does this change mean for me?" Seeking the answer to that question is a first step to figuring out the best path forward through the change. After that fateful day in February 2019, I had to find the courage to be an active participant in the change — navigating with my family through our new reality as a family of three and doing the work of healing and making sense of our loss. I couldn't just let it happen to me — that kind of passive response to painful change can leave us forever adrift and never truly in control again. I needed to be part of defining what the change — what William's death and all it required of us as a family — meant for me. That's what I (at first unknowingly) did when I took my leave of absence. I created space to learn and collaborate and lead again. I stopped time in my career so I could recapture it with my family.

The second lesson I took away from the earliest weeks and months of my grief is that change will often require a "letting go" of who you used to be. Change often exacts a loss of a part of yourself — of your identity. When a change is big enough, you won't be the same person on the other side. For me, that meant letting go of the piece of my identity that was so tightly wrapped around my career and this notion that being in constant motion was the only way to be. "Nick Shaw, ambitious business leader with a need to prove himself" was suddenly who I used to be, but not who I am. I had to let go of that former identity and default attitude; it was only through acceptance of this that I was able to give my full self to healing with Susie and Kai.

W.W.W.W.

What would he want?
Would he want me to join him ...
Would he want our union to dissolve ...
Would he want his best friend,
his little brother, to suffer?

No, he wouldn't want any of that.
He would want his love to flourish through us.
He would want his momma to smile again.
He would want his brother to grow up
and have the life he couldn't.
He would want me to write our story.

Noel

CHAPTER 5

I WROTE THE first draft of this chapter on the three-year anniversary of William's death, and the four W's that are the title of the poem (W.W.W.W. — What Would Willy Want?) mean as much to me today as they did back then. That huge but focused question — What would Willy want? — has served as a set of guiding principles that has helped me through some of the most difficult moments.

When we got home from Montana, the depths of my grief started to kick in. I had no idea what to expect. Most of the literature that exists on grief frames it as a neatly structured and linear process that one can expect to go through. My own experience of grief was anything but predictable, which made it even more challenging as I was constantly judging whether I was doing it the "right" way. Was I feeling the way I was supposed to? Was I progressing along the grieving process at the right pace? I now know that these questions are irrelevant, as the process of grief is intensely personal and a uniquely different experience for each person. But back then, I felt as if I were failing at it and my inner critic was doing his best to remind me of this.

In those early days, it felt like I would be carrying my grief around forever. I envisioned having a perpetual black cloud hanging over me, like in cartoons, dashing any hope of joy and happiness. As depressing as this was, part of me was OK with it. It was the only way I knew to keep William with me. If I stopped grieving, it would be as if William was no longer a part of my life … and that scared me to death. I couldn't stand the thought of losing him again, which meant that I was prepared for this deep level of grief to be with me for the rest of my days (or so I thought).

One day, I was in a particularly dark place emotionally. It was the second time during this black period that suicide infiltrated my thoughts. I could see no good options. I was sitting on the couch in my office, staring into nothingness. It all felt so hopeless, and I felt I couldn't do this for much longer. I wanted it all to stop and was ready to call it quits. Then — out of nowhere — a more hopeful notion found its way through the noise. It was faint at first but then it got louder. "What would Willy want?"

In those early days, it felt like I would be carrying my grief around forever.

Choosing Love Over Grief

William loved to love, and that love was deepest for his family — his mother, his father, and his little brother. One of his favorite ways to show this love was with a giant bear hug. When he hugged us, it was as if he was trying to squeeze us so tight that we'd know he was doing it with every ounce of love that he had in his body. From that same place of love, he would have wanted us — amidst this horrible situation — to find happiness. He wouldn't have wanted me to end my life early and he absolutely wouldn't have wanted more suffering for Susie and Kai. When you lose someone who you care so deeply about, initially you are so distraught that you don't immediately think about living your life in a way that honors theirs. You don't think about what their wishes would have been for how the people they loved should endure. What would Willy want us to do? How would he want us to live our lives?

Susie and I had heard the horror stories of what can happen when a family loses a child. Many times, the grief drives a wedge between the parents and the story ends in divorce, further adding to the trauma for any surviving children. Susie and I were determined not to let this happen; it's not what William would have wanted. Losing one life was enough and allowing three more lives to be ruined was not acceptable. It would be a dishonor to William, and it would have meant that his life and his death were meaningless. The mantra "What would Willy want?" became our guiding light and trusty compass to help us navigate uncharted waters. It was about the love that William had for us and the love that our family had for each other.

> ## The mantra "What would Willy want?" became our guiding light and trusty compass to help us navigate uncharted waters.

I, of course, had no delusions that this new way of thinking would magically make everything better and that suddenly my grieving process would end. The road that lay ahead would be long and one of the most challenging of my life. It would be filled with moments of intense pain, guilt and despair, and there was no way around it. I was learning that grief is not something any of us can avoid or circumvent. It's something we must face; the only way forward is to go through it. The "W.W.W.W." mantra has helped me so much as I have continued my process of grieving. I know it will continue to help me for the rest of my life. It is something I always have when I need it. In times of struggle, I just pose the question to the universe and, as if William were still with me, he always gives me a compassionate answer. My grief will always be with me, and that's OK. What I have come to realize is that, over time, grief becomes softer and gentler. It becomes easier to live with. And it makes it easier for *us* to live.

Silencing My Inner Critic

Not everyone has a story like mine. Maybe your tragedies have been of a different kind, or that you've avoided tragedy altogether ... so far. (Knock wood.) But whether our challenges are big or small, frequent or rare, what ties us together is the rollercoaster of highs and lows. Life is filled with a series of up and down moments. Over and over, twisting and turning, often speeding up or slowing down — taking us by surprise and sometimes taking our breath away.

Losing William has been the lowest moment I have had to face. While I am hopeful that I will never again experience anything even remotely as tragic, I know I will be tested in many other ways. The mantra — "What would Willy want?" — will help me persevere through whatever else life has to throw at me. In dark moments, it has given me something to turn to that allows me to feel less helpless. It has provided me with a way of reframing a challenging situation into something more positive and constructive. Because what Willy always wanted was something joyful or silly, loving or meaningful, exhilarating or adventurous. Often, when facing adversity, it can be very easy to quickly take on a more negative perspective. I am naturally more pre-disposed to go to the negative first (i.e., the glass is half empty). When I do this, I focus solely on the problem or issue that is challenging me. I stew on it, simmering in negative thoughts and feelings. I take on a victim mentality, surrendering to my fears; doing this incapacitates me, preventing me from acting in a more meaningful and intentional way.

But now I have a new way to reframe that kind of thinking. I ponder what my forever-nine-year-old son, William, would want if he were here to tell me. I have found — from my own experiences — and observed in the experiences of my colleagues, clients, and friends that when we reframe a challenging situation, the view from a different perspective enables us to be more "at choice" with our actions. We may still feel disappointed or dejected by what is happening to us, but we take a more proactive stance to finding a path forward to overcoming the challenge. Being "at peace" is accepting what is — and being "at choice" lets us behave and communicate in a way that creates a deeper peace. It's a subtle but meaningful shift in how I think about and live my life.

Since William's death, I have found myself in that dreaded negative place many times. When I'm there, feeling stuck, I become particularly hard on myself. I become my seven-year-old self, whose only defense mechanism is to become overly self-critical, doubting myself at every turn. Each time, I have had to remind myself of my mantra — of my question to supersede all questions — which quickly snaps me back to that more positive frame. What more positive framing is there than the love of your nine-year-old son just wanting the best for you? When I think about his wishes for my life and for our family, it's as if Willy is standing in front of me, urging me with all his might to find compassion for myself. He is giving me one of his signature hugs and his love is flowing right into me. With his love, I can flip the script and find the self-compassion that I need to persevere.

On my hardest days, it's still not easy. I think that most of us are naturally predisposed to being hard on ourselves, particularly in those dark moments. Because of this, self-compassion eludes us. Being gentle with ourselves feels foreign, indulgent, awkward, or even selfish. But being gentle with ourselves (instead of hard on ourselves) is exactly how we grow, heal, and move forward stronger.

If you find yourself in such a moment, please think of someone who loves you and ask yourself, "What would that the person want for me?" My hope is that you will be able to take the love and compassion that they have for you and turn it inward.

Love Manifest

Love is small green ribbons
affixed around town.

Love is a community
enveloping a grieving family.

Love is travelers near and far
coming to pay their respects.

Love is a moment of lucidity
amidst the fog.

Love is connecting
in a way you haven't before.

Love is a wife being strong
when her husband is falling apart.

Love is the smile on a six-year old's face
as he sees a picture of his brother.

Love is the pain I feel in my heart.
Love is the gift my son gave to the world.

Noel

CHAPTER 6

SOMEDAY, WE WILL die. It's the one universal shared experience of humanity. We are hardwired to accept this truth when it comes to loved ones — and even ourselves — if, and only if, a long life has been lived. All my grandparents have passed and while this was sad, it followed the natural order of things — which made it more acceptable. What we are less inclined to accept is that death sometimes comes for us when we have lived shorter lives — that sometimes "the good die young." When a child dies, there is no turning away from this reality. A life cut short is a stark reminder of our mortality. As harsh as this truth is, it also allows for one of the most beautiful aspects of humanity to emerge: love.

Until William died, I had never spent much time thinking about what love is. I had felt the intensity of love mostly in those moments of affection I shared with my family — when I said "I love you" to Susie for the first time or when I held each one of my children when they were born. While these are some of the ways that love can manifest, it can also manifest in so many more. When we got back to Carlisle from the trip to Big Sky, I experienced love in ways I had never imagined. I experienced it in acts both big and small, with people I knew well and with complete strangers. I felt it in the connection that people had with each other as they shared in the emotion of what had occurred. I realized that if you open your heart to it, love is everywhere.

When you lose a child, you become part of one of the only clubs no one ever wants to join. Interestingly, there is no name to describe someone who has lost a child — no term equivalent to "widow" or "orphan." You take on a status that is both undesirable and nameless. You are a statistical outlier (per the CDC, just 13.7 out of 1,000 children aged 5-14 die every year in the United States). In the wake of a child's death, you are now "those people" who others hope never to become, and you feel utterly alone. When we got back home to Carlisle, we didn't know how we would be received. What would people think of us? How would we be judged? After all, one of our main responsibilities as parents is to protect our children and we had failed to do this. Amidst everything else, this was yet another uncertainty we were facing: how other people would look at us, think of us, talk about us. We were about to become the talk of the town.

There is no name to describe someone who has lost a child — no term equivalent to "widow" or "orphan." You take on a status that is both undesirable and nameless.

Carlisle is a small, rural Massachusetts town with a population of approximately 5,000 people. It's a mostly residential community where the heart and soul of the town is our K-8 school. Carlisle is fortunate to have a very good school system, which draws young families to the town. Susie and I had become quite close to a lot of those families by virtue of our children becoming friends as they grew up together. In nearly every way, our kids were the focal point that brought the Carlisle community together.

This was different from what I had grown up with. I grew up in New York City and the concept of community was a foreign one to me. After school and work, we went home to our apartments, closed our doors, and lived our lives. People "minded their own business." As soon as the news spread about William's death, I experienced what true community is all about. The residents of Carlisle rallied in a way that I never could have imagined. The entire town embraced us with support and love. They were unified by our loss; our loss was their loss, because in a town that revolves around our collective kids, one local family losing a child hits close to home for many people. They say it takes a village to raise a child; it also takes a village to mourn one.

They say it takes a village to raise a child; it also takes a village to mourn one.

Showing Up, Again and Again

As you can imagine, Susie and I were exhausted and depleted from all
we had just endured, and now we had to begin planning how we would
honor William's life. As soon as we got home, people from all over town
began to stop by and pay their respects. Our home burst alive with activity
as we were determined to lay William to rest. His body was due to arrive
at the funeral parlor in the neighboring town, five days after we got home.
Immediately, our Carlisle friends and neighbors took matters into their
own hands, planning the funeral and figuring out how to honor William
in ways that would be inclusive to the children within the community.
People of all ages took on different projects.

Word got out that green was William's favorite color. Green ribbons were
affixed — by countless people from the town of Carlisle — to trees and
posts around town, creating a pathway from our house to the Unitarian
church where the funeral would take place. Because no one was sure
which route we would take to the church, they marked multiple different
routes. The funeral was on March 2, 2019, and — due to a storm the night
before — there was snow everywhere. It was a beautiful sight to see these
green ribbons against the white snow that had blanketed our town. Each
ribbon was a reminder of just how much people cared about us.

The funeral itself was a beautiful tribute to William. It was held in the
Unitarian church where Susie would take the boys on Sundays. The
church itself is quite small and every seat was filled. So many people came
that an overflow area had to be created on the bottom floor of the church,
where a live broadcast of the service was streamed. My brother Claude,
who is a gifted orator, gave an amazing eulogy that captured the essence
of who William was. My good friend Jim Memory also spoke and shared
some beautiful stories about William and some of the great memories
that we all had together. At the front of the church, by the casket, was
a poster-sized picture of William. In it, he is poking his head out of a fort
that he and his friends built with leaves and sticks, and his curly blond
hair combined with his pale skin makes him appear angelic. As I listened
to the service, all I could focus on through my tears was that picture.
There he was, looking at me, at my soul, with his caring and kind eyes.
I couldn't take my eyes off him.

The photo that was displayed next to the casket at the
funeral — William in a fort he built with his friends.

After the funeral, hundreds of people — both from our town and friends
and family from afar — congregated at a reception held at the school.
They served BBQ turkey legs because it was one of William's favorite
foods. No detail was too small to ignore in how William was honored and
remembered.

Having a community like Carlisle behind us helped us to feel less alone in
our worst moments. Even after the funeral was over, our town continued
to help us, providing us with meals as well as taking turns doing our
laundry well into the summer months. People from all over town wanted
to contribute however possible. They seemed to understand that our
struggles would not end after the funeral — that we were just beginning
to process our grief and navigate life as a smaller, forever-changed family.
Susie and I will forever be grateful to the Carlisle community for how they
took care of us in our darkest of hours.

Our family and friends also showed up in countless ways that demonstrated their love for us and for William. My best friend, Alan, who I have
known since kindergarten, was the first person at our house every day

and the last person to leave in the evening, making sure we were properly taken care of. He drove us to the funeral. My twin brother, Claude, arrived five days before the funeral, and was up in the wee hours of the night with me when I couldn't sleep. We sat at our kitchen counter recounting stories of William so that he could write the most memorable eulogy possible. My older sister, Caroline, in the true spirit of her astrological symbol (Taurus), was as persistent as a bull chasing a matador, calling me every day for months to check up on me and make sure I was OK. Susie's family — her mother and father and her brother, John, and his wife, Erin — were there for us at every turn, holding us up with their love.

Nick (right) with brother Claude and sister Caroline.

People came from across the globe to pay their respects and to demonstrate their love. A friend was en route to Japan for a business trip and as soon as he heard the news, canceled his trip while laying over between flights. Another friend, who was stationed in Germany with the armed forces, flew back to the U.S. for two days to be there for us. When I was at the reception, everywhere I turned were people from different parts of my life — college friends, current and former colleagues, ex-bosses, the Uber driver who I would call to give me rides to the airport for my business trips. I was truly touched by people's willingness to be there for us. Amidst this outpouring of love, two moments stood out that touched me deeply. One involved my mother and the other my father.

Words I Needed to Hear

My mother always provided me with emotional support as a child. When I struggled with my issues of inferiority, she was always there for me. She made it her mission to help me overcome these challenges. Now, in the most harrowing experience of my life, I was not able to turn to her. My mother had been diagnosed with Alzheimer's disease several years before and by 2019 was at a stage where she couldn't really handle basic tasks anymore. Several days before William's funeral, my phone rang and when I picked it up, I was surprised to hear my mother's voice. Somehow, amidst the fog of her condition, she managed to pick up the phone and be there for me just as she always had been. She told me how sorry she was about what had happened and then just listened to me and gave me space to share how I was feeling.

Toward the end of the call, she told me how much she loved William and that he will always be in her heart. Then she told me how much she loved me. It was the first time in a long time she was the mother I had known and loved when I was a boy. It is perhaps one of the last lucid conversations she had with me. As I write this book, she is still alive but incapable of having a conversation. It was a small miracle of love that allowed us to have one last meaningful moment together. I needed that conversation more than I can truly express.

As it turned out, the loss of William would also give rise to a powerful interaction with my father. My dad comes from an entire generation of men who were raised not to share their emotions. And his personal experiences made him doubly sober and emotionally guarded. At an early age, my dad and his family fled their home in Croatia to avoid being captured by the Nazis in World War II. He had to learn how to survive. In response to facing such adversity in his formative years, my father adopted stoicism as his way of tackling the peaks and valleys of life. He took on a very practical approach to life — focusing on what he could control and letting go of what he couldn't. Through this approach, he embodied the

American dream. He and his family lost everything as a result of the war but, through his hard work and determination, he achieved immense success as one of the top management consultants at the premier firm, McKinsey & Company. His practical, less-than-emotional approach to life and work has served him relatively well. But I realize that not outwardly expressing your emotions is not the same thing as not *having* emotions. Like everyone, my father feels deeply.

The loss of his grandson, of course, deeply affected my father and, though he will never admit it, grappling with the associated emotions must have been challenging for him. The challenge was perhaps most difficult for him when he and I would speak while I was in an emotional state. On one such occasion, he said something I will never forget. In his practical way he said, "I hope you know this goes without saying but I would trade places with William in a second."

Even now, as I type those words, it brings tears to my eyes. I love my father very much and I know he loves me. He just conveys this in his own way. That moment was one of the very few times in my adult life that I felt a deep emotional connection to my father. In that moment, his love manifested for me in a very different way than it ever had before.

•   •   •

Love, which is such a deep part of our humanity, doesn't have to be reserved exclusively for the most sensational moments of our lives. It can thrive beyond the magnificent and the tragic, if we allow it to. Love can flourish in our everyday interactions and our mundane moments. We are bound together by our shared humanity. The problem is that we forget this sometimes. We forget that inside most of us is a longing to love and be loved. We let our ego-driven fears determine how we see others, often subsuming or diminishing their humanity.

We forget that inside most of us is a longing to love and be loved.

If we could just remind ourselves — when we are engaging with another — that "there stands another human being." Someone like me. Someone who, likely, shares the same basic needs as I do. Someone who will be filled with happiness when something great happens and someone who will be devastated by a tragic loss. If we could remember this and open ourselves to others, acts of love and kindness would abound. This can happen on a small scale, when one person engages another. It can also happen on a large scale, just as the Carlisle community demonstrated when they enveloped my family with their love in our darkest of hours.

What If?

What if time
hadn't stopped
on a chair in the sky?

Or a turn
down this path
was a turn
down another?

What if that tree
in the woods
was two
inches away ...

Or if ten feet in front
was two feet behind?

What if? What
if? What if?

I could ask
this question
in
countless more ways
but always to no avail.

This confluence
of events —
so random and
insignificant —
conspired to create
that singular moment.

So hard to accept
with a rational mind,
whose aim for control
makes it all seem
so bearable.

No matter
how many times
I revisit "what if,"
I always come back to
it was meant to be.

Noel

CHAPTER 7

THE QUESTION "WHAT if?" — when forward looking — is
filled with wonder and possibility. It explores what could be and enables
you to think outside the box that frames your current reality. If asked at
the right time, it can open a wider view to someone who needs stretch-
ing to transform their lives. I use this question a lot to help my clients
envision a different (and better) future. Using the question when looking
backward also has its merits. An exploration of the past through a lens
of "what if?" can teach us a great deal. What if we had done things differently? Would we have gotten a different outcome? "What if" is a way to
process what happened and, hopefully, to learn to do things differently,
better, or more deliberately next time. In the business world, a thoughtful
"what if" session after a big project, milestone, or crisis is often referred to
as a "postmortem" and I have conducted many such sessions with teams
to help them learn from experience. I never would have imagined that
I would be conducting a literal postmortem, as I attempted to determine
what happened to William, by incessantly asking, "What if?"

In the minutes, hours, and days after William died, one particular "what
if" question consumed my thoughts: What if I had done more when I was
searching for William? The embankment off the slope that William skied
into was filled with trees in deep powder snow. These conditions create
a phenomenon called "tree wells." A tree well is an area of deep, uncon-
solidated snow around the base of a tree that can "swallow" a skier if they
come too close to the tree trunk.[1] When people fall into tree wells, they
are buried — often to their chests or entirely — and can die of suffocation

---

[1] For readers unfamiliar with skiing and with tree wells, I recommend watching this brief
video to better understand this part of our story: https://www.tetongravity.com/video/ski/
psa-tree-wells-are-dangerous-and-how-to-avoid-getting-stuck-in-them.

or exposure. When I tried to search for William, I fell into a tree well after only a couple steps into the woods. I sunk to my chest in powder and the snow was so heavy that it felt as if I were encased in concrete. It took all my strength just to pull myself out, tugging on the branches of the trees that surrounded me. Once free from the tree well, I realized that searching through the trees alone was too dangerous. I was forced to retreat and find another way.

The thought that William suffered while being trapped in a tree well, alone and afraid, was tearing me apart. It consumed my thoughts in the days after we returned home. I tried to recreate what had happened to see if things could have been different. My head was constantly flooded with questions; I was searching for impossible answers. Could I have done more to save him? If I had gotten to him in time, would he be alive today? In the days after the accident, my thirst for answers was insatiable. Like an addict whose weakness is emotional catastrophizing, I needed my next fix — my next journey into "what if" — and I kept going back for more … no matter how much this tormented me. I was desperate to find answers. Fortunately, this would be one of the few "what ifs" that would have a resolution. About a week or so after the accident, I finally got some reprieve when we received the coroner's autopsy report. Per the report, William had died instantly from blunt force trauma to the head and chest. There is nothing I could have done to save him. Most importantly, he didn't suffer.

> ## My head was constantly flooded with questions; I was searching for impossible answers.

Examining Every Detail

The news from the coroner, helpful as it was, only provided me with momentary relief. There were still so many unanswered questions and my rational brain's need for answers soon returned to overdrive. I examined every little detail to see if any slight change here or there could have led to a different outcome.

What if I hadn't made a wrong turn? We would have gone down a different slope and likely, I wouldn't be writing this book. The problem is that I did make a wrong turn. It was an honest mistake — one that I have made countless times. One that all skiers make. At that moment, that simple mistake seemed like nothing, but it led to the direst of consequences.

What if instead of being in front of him, I was behind him? I will never know what caused William to veer off course and into the woods but, even if I'd been behind him, I don't think I could have prevented it. Something caused him to veer suddenly and ski off the side of the catwalk and into the woods. Because there were never any tracks in the woods, my only conclusion is that he was airborne when he hit the tree, which means he was going pretty fast. Whatever happened, me being behind him wouldn't have made a difference. I would have seen him die and I'm not sure that would have been better than how the events actually transpired.

What if his trajectory while airborne took him two feet to the right, or if the tree itself were two feet in a different direction? According to Matt, who found him, it was a matter of 12 inches this way or that way and things could have ended differently.

What if the previous year, William and I hadn't gotten stuck on the chairlift, and we had made it to the top of Lone Peak? Would we have been as eager to go there again on this day in 2019 or might we have gone on a different day with an entirely different set of circumstances?

What if?

As I continued to run the events of February 19th over in my head — to see if anything could have been done differently — I began to realize that the answer was "no." What happened to William was, by its very definition, a "freak accident" — one that could not have been predicted nor prevented. If I had taken William down a riskier run and he had fallen to his death, in some way the accident would have made sense. My poor judgment would have been responsible, but that wasn't the case. William was an experienced and able skier and was skiing on perhaps the easiest type of slope there is. He was wearing his ski helmet which is a "MUST" in our family. I can honestly say, were that day to happen again, I wouldn't have done anything differently given the same set of circumstances. It's one of the most difficult things I have had to come to grips with because I so desperately wanted to feel like I could have prevented the tragedy. Even though I couldn't turn back time, the awful possibility that I could have prevented the accident seemed to offer a tiny sense of control over an uncontrollable tragedy.

No matter how hard I tried to explain how this could have happened, I had to recognize that all these small and seemingly insignificant moments were randomly stitched together. For some reason this set of events, actions, circumstances, conditions, and decisions came together in such a way that William died, almost as if it were simply inevitable. Asking "what if" in this context proved to be a useless exercise and only served one purpose: to create a false sense of control. If I could figure out a rationale for what happened, then I could control it the next time. The next time? Why does that matter? Nothing I can do will bring William back. No amount of "what ifs" will give me the power to reverse what happened. What happened was meant to be. And, after countless hours of obsessive replay, that is the best I have been able to come up with.

Controlling the Uncontrollable

I am a control freak. I like to know how things will unfold; certainty brings me the comfort I need to feel safe in this world. The problem is that control is an illusion. We can try to plan, and we can try to make the best possible decisions to keep ourselves and our loved ones safe but, in the end, there will always be forces beyond our control that might intervene. Everything that happened to us on February 19, 2019, is a prime example of this. It was a day that began like any other but ended in an unlikely and tragic way. I say "unlikely" because the probability of it happening was extremely low. What is the probability of all those different and subtle events coming together to create that outcome? To get to the tram that takes you to the top of Lone Peak, William and I had to take the same chairlift we had gotten stuck on the year before. Ironically, we had a conversation about the probability of getting stuck on it again. In hindsight, it's eerie that we had this conversation about an improbable event. It's as if it were some kind of strange foreshadowing of the improbable event that would occur not even two hours later.

We can't control everything and, for me, the lesson in that is that perhaps we shouldn't try so hard. If we could just loosen our grip, even a bit, perhaps life would feel a bit less constrained. When we try to exert control, we close ourselves off to what's possible and, when we do that, positive, optimistic "what if" scenarios of a more meaningful life elude us. It's only through acceptance of what life throws our way that we can really do this. Accept what occurs and look for the possibility that may unfold as a result. Too much time agonizing over "what if" for our past can prevent us from the positive possibilities when we think about "what if" for our future.

> **We can't control everything and, for me, the lesson in that is that perhaps we shouldn't try so hard. If we could just loosen our grip, even a bit, perhaps life would feel a bit less constrained.**

Polarities

As tears of joy flood my heart,
a sadness so deep stakes its claim.

Emotions at war, neither side gives an inch,
deploy strategies of guilt to conquer the prize.

Two souls intertwined as death creates life,
such that no flip of a coin can bring resolution.

Honoring them both is the only way forward ...
to call a truce and bring peace within.

CHAPTER 8

OUR THIRD SON, Bodhi Soren Shaw, was born on July 28, 2020. It was an arduous and anxiety-filled delivery because Bodhi had been diagnosed with an intralobar pulmonary sequestration, a rare birth defect. During one of the prenatal scans, the doctor noticed extra tissue had formed within our new baby's lungs. This tissue was being fed by a blood vessel but served no other purpose. The main concern with this condition is that it can lead to infection later in life. The normal course of action is to remove the excess tissue via surgery. But first we needed to welcome him into the world. The more immediate concern during delivery was what the impact of this lung condition would be on the baby's breathing once he was out of the womb and breathing on his own. To make matters more complicated, Bodhi's position during delivery would require the use of forceps to pull him out. It all seemed overwhelming.

But we were in good hands, and there were a lot of doctors there to assist. Because we were in a teaching hospital, several residents were present to observe the procedure. With the standard labor and delivery team, a team from the neonatal intensive care unit (NICU), and the extra observers, there must have been 15 people crowding the small delivery room, which added a sense of chaos to an already anxious situation. We had already lost one son and all I could think about was that we might lose another. Fortunately, nine minutes after Susie began pushing, Bodhi emerged and cried out with all his force, letting everyone know — in no uncertain terms — that his lungs were functioning just fine. After a brief period with the NICU team, Bodhi was eventually laid on Susie's chest. Susie and I looked at each other, both crying tears of happiness. We immediately FaceTimed Kai, who was suddenly an 8-year-old big brother, and for first time since William died, our family felt more in balance.

Nick and Susie celebrate the arrival of baby Bodhi.

Later that day, when we transitioned to the post-partem room, I was able to hold Bodhi for the first time. As he was sleeping on my chest, I thought to myself how amazing this was and that I wouldn't trade this for anything else in the world. Just as the thought entered my mind, another thought floored me. Bodhi was born because William died. Had that tragedy not occurred, then the miracle that is Bodhi would not have occurred. My eldest and youngest sons, who have never met, will forever be inextricably linked, as the death of one led to the life of another. The challenge for me was how to hold both. How can there be room for happiness amidst such pain and despair? The answer to that question is a challenge that Susie and I had both grappled with many times as we processed our grief, especially that first year.

No Feelings Felt Right

For the first six years of his life, Kai was our family's "little brother" — taught by and loved by his big brother, William. Every day, Kai woke up to a world in which he had two loving parents to guide him and an older brother to show him the way. So, how does a second grader cope with the loss of his big brother? We had no guidebooks for how to properly help Kai through this difficult odyssey. We were all trying to figure it out together with the help of our family therapist. There were a lot of unknowns but the one thing that Susie and I were clear about is that Kai was our priority.

In the months after William died, Susie and I did everything we could to give Kai a "normal" life. We traveled a lot while I was on my leave of absence from work, and the trips we took allowed us to get a change of scenery and, more importantly, to create some new and happy memories for Kai. We did succeed in creating those memories, but I personally found it difficult to stay "in the moment" while we went on living. Any time a moment of happiness would occur, my despair would tug at me. Whether we were having a new experience on an air boat in the Everglades, playing with our new puppy, Marmalade, on the beach, or wearing ridiculous blow-up sumo wrestler costumes for Halloween, that deep feeling of despair would always appear. It's as if the feeling itself were fighting for its own survival, imploring me not to forget it. My despair wanted so much to be part of my life that it did anything it could to remind me of its existence. Whether I was happy or sad, I was unable to fully be in either state without feeling intense guilt. In those happy moments, it was about feeling the guilt of moving forward without William. In those sad moments, I felt guilty for not being able to be fully present for those around me, particularly Kai. There was no solace no matter what I was doing or how I was feeling. After Bodhi was born, these feelings only intensified.

> **I personally found it difficult to stay "in the moment" while we went on living. Any time a moment of happiness would occur, my despair would tug at me.**

It was a very difficult place to be. I could never be at ease with how I was feeling. No matter how I felt, it felt wrong. I didn't want to be this way for the rest of my life. It reminded me of someone who Susie and I had met at a grief group. We had found a group that met in a neighboring town and decided to attend an early evening session. When we got to the group, we realized that in addition to Susie and me, there were only two other people — a moderator and another attendee. The moderator was an older gentleman. He kicked off the session by sharing his story, and he ended with a sentiment that I will never forget. He said that since the death of his daughter, there wasn't a day that went by when he was able to be happy. The way he said it made me cringe. He looked at his daughter's death like a judge handing down a life sentence: you take what you get, you accept it, and you do your time. As novices to grief, this was a tough thing for Susie and me to hear. It didn't send the most inspiring message and, as a result, we never went back to that group. We didn't know the ideal way forward, but I think we both realized that forgoing happiness for the rest of our lives was not the future we wanted to create for ourselves or for Kai.

Gun shy after that first "grief group" experience, we still knew it would be best to find community through our bereavement and we eventually joined another grief group that better served our needs. The one benefit of that experience — of meeting the father who hadn't lived a single happy day since his child's death — was that it gave me a model for how I did not want to be. We had lost William, but we had two young boys to raise — a child who had also endured the trauma of William's death and deserved not to be defined by it, and a new baby who deserved to be protected from the systemic grief that could have consumed us if we let it. We needed to heal. I wanted to heal. Yet when I held Bodhi, I longed to hold William. How could I hold them both?

Reconciling the Irreconcilable

For as long as I can remember, my life has been a big comparison game: good/bad, better/worse, winning/losing. And I know I'm not alone in this, because it's a universal human tendency to compare and categorize things. We always want to place things in well-defined boxes to make sense of them. It's our way of simplifying and processing all the input we take in and doing it sometimes in a fraction of a second. Our shared ability to categorize and stereotype is what has allowed our species to survive and evolve by determining what is a threat and what isn't. "Either that thing in front of me will kill me or it won't." As a result, we tend to frame things as "either/or."

I've understood the either/or game since early in my childhood. As a fraternal twin, I often heard and witnessed people comparing me and my brother. Most people hear the word "twin," and they think "the same." But when people saw my brother and me, they couldn't reconcile that we could be so different. Their only way to rationalize this was to compare and categorize us. For me, as the more vertically challenged and slightly chubbier of the two, I often had to accept being at the lesser end of the continuum on which my brother and I were being compared. I was exposed to this way of thinking a lot as a child. Eventually, I fell into a pattern of always judging myself and the world in this very black and white "either/or" way. When we do this, we begin to see the world as a series of dichotomies — a never-ending choice between two polar opposites. Fat or fit, smart or dumb, shy or outgoing, good or bad, past or present, happy or sad.

When William died and I eventually tried to be happy again, I discovered that this "either/or" thinking didn't work for me anymore. I would try to make a choice between being sad about something (like William's birthday or a fun new experience with Kai and/or Bodhi), or being happy about it. But often, I was both. A choice between the polar opposite feelings couldn't be made; "either/or" simply wasn't possible. Contrary to everything I had always thought to be true, equal and opposite feelings, mindsets, and attitudes can and do exist at the same time.

So, how do we resolve the irreconcilable? It's a bit of a trick question because, by its very nature if something, is irreconcilable, then it can't be reconciled. In my mind and in my heart, I had been trying to fight the coexistence of happiness and grief. I had been trying to tell myself that it's not possible (or at least not preferable) to be happy and sad at the same time — that somehow, I was always either dishonoring William's memory or diminishing the present moment with Kai, Bodhi, and Susie. But that's simply not true. Instead of trying to resolve these competing forces and feelings, I finally realized that I can simply stop trying. Instead of forcing the choice between the two opposites, I simply don't choose. To do this, I stopped framing concepts as "either/or" and started framing them as an "and."

This was the space I had to eventually reach when dealing with the two competing states of my psyche. I had to be able to hold both my despair *and* my happiness at the same time. I had to accept that I could be happy *and* sad at the same time. I could revel in the delight of holding my newborn son *and* at the same time be devastated by the loss of my oldest son. I could delight in sharing new and exciting experiences with Kai *and* at the same time be shattered by the fact that I will never be able to share those same experiences with William. I had to let go of a rigid way of seeing the world and make room for possibility. I had to stop letting one feeling diminish the other; I made room for both feelings to coexist. The more I am conscious about the fact that our feelings don't have to be mutually exclusive, the easier it is for me to navigate my life. Holding space for the polarities in my life has been a challenge and I'm still a work in progress — this is not something that comes naturally to me. But choosing to live in the acceptance of "and" has allowed me to appreciate each moment — and the feelings that may come with it — more fully.

I had to let go of a rigid way of seeing the world and make room for possibility.

The Pride of a Father,
the Pride of a Son

On that day as I watched you
take on the Mountain's challenge
with a boldness and confidence I hadn't seen before,
I was in awe at seeing you break through
and win the battle over Thanos, your fear personified.

As a father, these were the moments
I had dreamt about the first day I held you.
All those firsts that you would conquer.
Seeing you get lost in the thing I loved most ...
a feeling so overwhelming it touched me to my core.

And when it was all over,
you came to me in a dream and said
"I am as proud of you as you are of me."
You have been teaching this to me since the day
you were born.
Make me proud, Dad ... show me the way.

CHAPTER 9

IT WASN'T UNTIL almost three years after William's accident that I finally watched the video I had taken of him skiing on that day. I had taken the USB drive containing the video and tucked it into a drawer, not quite sure if I would ever be able to watch it. I was afraid of what it might stir in me — the pain it might evoke. Then, as the three-year anniversary drew near, I realized that as time had gone by, that I was starting to feel too removed from everything that had happened. I found myself not thinking as often about William and dedicating less time to actively trying to connect with him.

Since that fateful day in February 2019, a lot had happened in my life, my career, my family, and my marriage. After six months of bereavement leave, I went back to work full-time in the fall of 2019. Shortly thereafter, Bodhi joined our family in the summer of 2020 — during the COVID-19 pandemic. So much was going on in our lives during the three years that followed William's death that, when I stepped back and looked at it objectively, I could see that it was understandable that my attention was diverted elsewhere. But I didn't like the way it made me feel.

A part of me was missing, so I committed to re-establishing my connection with William. In December of 2021, Susie took Bodhi and Kai to her parents' house for a couple of days, leaving me with some much-needed time to myself. I decided to dedicate a day to connecting with William. I spent some time at the cemetery and then went on a mountain bike ride on one of the trails that William and I often rode together. I stopped at a spot where we often took a snack break. It's nestled in a grove of tall oak trees that sit atop a small hill and form a semi-circle. About 50 feet away from the ridge is a beautiful pond that shimmers deep within the forest. It is a perfect little oasis where William and I would spend some quiet moments together, recharging for the remainder of our ride. Now, I desperately wanted to feel that connection again and I looked up at the sky and asked William aloud, "I feel so disconnected from you. Why are you so far away?"

William and Nick on an
autumn biking adventure.

William enjoying a rest at an oak grove
during a biking trip with his dad.

I had done this a lot in the early days after his death. I would put a question out there and often a response would come back to me. What came back to me on this day is "You have to work at it." If I wanted to connect with William, I would have to do it in an active way — as opposed to hoping that it would happen on its own. I knew what I had to do. When I got back home, I sat in William's room and, after some initial hesitation, I watched the video of his last run down the bowls of Lone Peak on the day he died. I wrote the poem at the beginning of this chapter right after watching it.

An Epic Run

Watching the video was a first step in reconnecting with some feelings that I hadn't felt in a while. The GoPro video camera I had used had been strapped to my chest and the footage follows William as he skis down the slope. GoPro cameras are designed for extreme outdoor activities and capturing fast-paced motion. Watching the footage gives you the sensation that you are right in the middle of the action. When I watched the video, I was transported back in time. There I was again on that mountain, following William having the run of his life. I was mesmerized by the motion of his nine-year-old body, the way he zig-zagged across the slope, picking up speed and then — with a flick of his hips — spun his skis and turned in the reverse direction. With each turn, you could hear an audible "CRUNCH" as his ski edges dug into the snow, fighting the inertia of his momentum, and then "SWOOSH" as he zipped back across the slope. There was a fluidity to how he moved, almost as if he were on a pendulum — swinging back and forth. Just when he got to the maximum point of the upswing, gravity would pull him back across the mountain. CRUNCH, SWOOSH, CRUNCH, SWOOSH.

William skiing down the mountain, fearless and joyful, taking his "one shot."

William was fearless and relentless as he took on the mountain. There were moments where he fell and recovered as if nothing had happened, which hadn't always been the case for William. At one point in the video, I catch up to him and ask him, "How's it going?" His answer: "EPIC!" He was so at ease with himself.

William was fearless and relentless as he took on the mountain.

There was a time in William's short life when any setback that he faced was enough to demoralize him and make him quit. He was active and involved, but quick to give up. I recall one occasion when we made a long trip for William to compete in a cyclocross bike race. He was eight at the time and, in his heat, he was competing with kids as old as 16. Because he was so much smaller, he got lapped by some of the older kids. His frustration got the best of him, and he stormed off the track crying. It was a tough moment for me to witness. I felt terrible for him but also disappointed that he had reacted in this way. Like most parents, I always want to see my kids push through the difficult moments — but, on that day, William couldn't do it.

Eventually, through work with a therapist, he developed strategies to combat this. He learned to personify his fear by giving it a name. If the fear had a name, he could address it — head on — instead of grappling with an abstract presence in his life. The name he gave his fear was Thanos, the archrival and villain in one of William's favorite Marvel Avengers movies. On that final day of his life, skiing Lone Peak, William not only met the mountain's challenge but also won the battle over Thanos. With his fear gone, he was fully absorbed in the glory of doing one of his favorite things. He loved to ski, and he especially loved skiing well. It's exactly how I had felt so many times when I skied. Seeing him on that video made me feel more connected to him than ever. It was a reminder of how proud I am of him for how far he had come. What a gift to have that experience preserved forever on video.

My Pride and Joy, My Sons

There have been many instances when I have been overwhelmingly proud of my sons. Pride is a powerful emotion, particularly when it comes to our children. It has a way of warming our hearts and our souls. On one hand, it's about the happiness we feel as we see our children thriving. On the other hand, it's about the difference each child has made in our life. I remember a very specific conversation I had with William one day as I was taking him to ski practice. We were in my truck and, as was always the case, we were listening to music. On this occasion, we were listening to the *Hamilton* soundtrack. He asked me what my favorite song on the album was and I responded that it was "Dear Theodosia." The song is an ode by two of the main characters in the musical, Aaron Burr and Alexander Hamilton, to their respective children. There is a verse that I think best describes the pride I feel toward my sons. In it, Alexander Hamilton is telling his son, Philip, how proud he is of him.

> *Oh Philip, when you smile I am undone*
> *My son, look at my son*
> *Pride is not the word I'm looking for*
> *There is so much more inside me now*

Our children fill us up in ways that — before having them — we never could have imagined. Pride is the manifestation of our overflowing love for them. In that conversation with William, I told him why this was my favorite song and that it had to do with how proud I was of him and how proud I was to be his father. That conversation happened several weeks before he died. I am grateful that I was able to have it with him.

Our children fill us up in ways that — before having them — we never could have imagined. Pride is the manifestation of our overflowing love for them.

As parents, we naturally have a lot of pride in our children. But until William passed away, it never dawned on me that our kids have pride for us too. Often when a loved one passes, they may come back to visit us in our dreams. Many people refer to these dreams as visits or visitations. A characteristic of these visits is how vivid they are, as well as the fact that there is communication between you and the loved one you lost. Before William died, I was never really a spiritual person, nor did I believe in any type of afterlife. While I am still not sure where I lie on the topic of an afterlife, I can attest to the realness of these visits.

The most vivid visit happened a month after William left us. In the dream, I was searching for William just as I had been that day on the mountain.

Then, out of nowhere, William appeared, and we gave each other a huge hug that seemed to last forever. I told him how happy I was to see him, and he responded with the following, "I am happy to see you, but I can't stay. It's a shame because I am as proud of you as you are of me." It was a powerful moment to have my son tell me he was proud of me. In some ways, I believe he was preparing me for the tough road that lay ahead, wanting for me what I had always wanted for him — to persevere and conquer my own Thanos.

• • •

When it comes to our kids, pride is a two-way street — our pride for them and their pride for us. As parents, a big part of our job is forming human beings who, hopefully, will go on to lead productive and purposeful lives. As we watch them grow up, who they become is a direct reflection on us. Like mirrors, our kids reflect to us who we are — for better or for worse. Our kids look up to us as their role models and want to be proud of us. They watch our every move and take cues for how to be in this world. They mimic us because our behavior is sometimes the only reference point they have. Being a father of sons, I am greatly aware of just how much they look to me as their primary model for what it means to be a man and a father. That's not to say they won't have other role models (there may be teachers, coaches, aunts, uncles, older siblings, grandparents, neighbors, and others) but in those early years as they develop, we — as parents — are who they look to first.

Like mirrors, our kids reflect to us who we are — for better or for worse.

It's an unbelievable privilege to be a parent because we get to literally shape a life (sometimes more than one!). With this privilege comes the responsibility of being intentional about how we show up for our kids because of the enormous influence we have on them. That said, we don't have to be perfect. When we do falter, it's important that we own up to it. This shows our kids that we are not infallible, that it's OK to be vulnerable, and that we are simply human.

One family, three incarnations. (Far left) Susie and Nick with Kai and William. (Center) Susie and Nick with Kai. (Far right) Susie and Nick with Kai and Bodhi.

I often thought of William as the 2.0 version of me. The upgrade. As parents, we want our kids to be better than us and it is our responsibility to help make this happen. We want them to evolve in ways we haven't (or in ways that took us a long while to achieve or appreciate). We need to constantly push ourselves to learn and grow so that our kids can benefit from this and not repeat the same mistakes we have made. A big part of my life's purpose is "to learn so I can teach." My objective is to not only do this for the benefit of my clients but also for my kids. I realized what my purpose was in a meditation that my mentor suggested I do. He instructed me to sit and meditate and silently ask what my life purpose was ... and then just listen. I was to repeat the question every so often until an answer was revealed. I was skeptical at first, but as I sat there and repeated the question, what emerged first surprised me. In my mind, I had framed the exercise in the context of my career, but what came to me was that my most important "clients" were my sons. I needed to learn so I could teach them. I needed to do my own inner work so that my own limiting beliefs and habits wouldn't be adopted by them. Witnessing William overcome his insecurities — something that has taken me a lifetime to do for myself — made me immensely proud. I was proud because he was conquering his fears. Proud because history wasn't going to repeat itself.

Kai, in his own right, has also made me proud. As I write this book, Kai is now 11, two years older than William ever was, and as I watch him grow up and experience the moxie with which he faces the challenges of our tragedy and life in general, I am in awe of his ability to bounce back and move forward. Bodhi, too, makes me proud in his own cute and cuddly way. At three years old, he is a force to be reckoned with as he makes sense of this great big world he now lives in. While he can certainly be a challenge — as he is squarely in the "terrible twos" (and threes!) stage — watching him develop into a little person amazes me every day.

While parental pride can certainly manifest in those grand moments of accomplishment, it can also emerge in the little moments. We just need to be present and pay attention. We must be open to the all-important lessons that our kids can teach us. In what ways are they handling certain situations that might inform how we could handle them ourselves? In what ways are they emulating us that might cause us to reflect on our own behaviors — either good or bad? All three of my sons have pushed (and continue to push) me to be a better person because of the lessons they have taught me. It's ironic that I am *learning* from them so that I can *teach* them. I guess it's what evolution is all about: a self-reinforcing positive cycle of learning. And love.

We must be open to the all-important lessons that our kids can teach us.

The Wolf's Path

He walks alone at times,
finding his way in this world,
struggling to find his place in the pack.
He is paralyzed as he ponders
"Who should I be, how should I be?"

As he tumbles and flips through the hurdles within
and finds the boldness of a flat-brimmed hat,
he lets the rhythm of the music be his guide.
Inspired by a Founding Father,
he won't throw away his shot.

Turning compassion for others toward self —
strength found in his own authenticity.
"Be Yourself" became his mantra.
His gait more self-assured,
the pack now looks to him on how to be.

CHAPTER 10

A BIG PART of our journey during this lifetime is finding our place in this world. Who we want to be and how we want to be. It's a process that begins in childhood and gets refined as we continue to develop as adults. William was just beginning his own journey. I mentioned earlier that William had battled with anxiety and sometimes I wonder if part of his anxiety came from grappling with his own sense of who he was. I only come to this conclusion because, after a year of therapy, William had begun to be more comfortable with who he was, and his anxiety seemed to abate. He started to be OK with defining his own path, and a core element was simply allowing himself to be himself.

His desire to simply be himself was something he realized one Sunday at the Unitarian church in our town. Susie would take the kids to church on Sundays and part of the service included different activities for kids. One of the activities they did in the fall of 2017 was to set an intention for the coming year and write it down on a notecard. On William's notecard, written in bold red marker, was the phrase "BE YOURSELF!" He was almost eight at the time, and this simple phrase quickly became his mantra. I didn't appreciate the significance of it then, but looking back, I now realize that he fully embraced this.

Charting His Own Path

As we entered the new year, William was starting to gain more and more confidence. He began charting his own path — a path I think of as "a wolf's path." William's middle name is Wolfgang, in honor of my maternal grandfather. Wolfgang, in German, means "the wolf's path" and like wolves who sometimes leave their packs before either creating their own pack or finding another, William started to do things in his own way as opposed to following the mainstream. He was very athletic but never took to the more traditional ball sports like soccer, basketball, or baseball. He gravitated toward sports that were more individual in nature and blended elements of physical prowess and agility, as well as fostered a unique sense of style. He had started ski racing the year before but the sport that really piqued his interest was parkour. The aim of parkour is to get through an obstacle course in the most fluid way possible by using your body. It requires you to run, climb, flip, and tumble over and under different obstacles. He attended class once a week and, at home, we could hear the "thump, thump" of him practicing different moves over our heads in the third-floor playroom. He was good at it and his natural abilities — combined with his drive to put in the time to practice — were starting to show. He competed in his first parkour event in the fall of 2018 and made it past the initial rounds of the competition. This was a big step for him as he was starting to better manage the anxiety that came with performing.

William in his element as a new parkour competitor.

As he continued to find his way, William started to develop his own sense of style. He modeled it after one of the parkour teachers he looked up to. I remember being in the airport on the way to Big Sky and looking at William. There he was — with his skinny black jeans, a hooded sweatshirt, a pair of Vans, and a flat-brimmed hat. As I looked, I thought, "My kid looks really cool," almost envious of his style. He looked so at ease with who he was. It was another moment of fatherly pride, being able to see my son coming into his own.

> There he was — with his skinny black jeans, a hooded sweatshirt, a pair of Vans, and a flat-brimmed hat. As I looked, I thought, "My kid looks really cool," almost envious of his style. He looked so at ease with who he was.

While William was becoming more in tune with his body and his athleticism, he was also expanding his horizons in terms of his intellectual and creative pursuits and began to develop a deep interest in music. He took guitar lessons and he and I had a chance to play "Here Comes the Sun" by the Beatles together in a small recital his teacher organized. He would don a large pair of over-the-ear headphones as he sampled different music genres. On Saturdays, when we were at one of Kai's soccer or baseball games, we would often see William sitting on a fence, all on his own, getting lost in whatever music was playing. His taste in music was wide-ranging. Together, he and I would rock out to "Thunder Struck" by ACDC to get pumped up before ski races. With Susie, he loved to listen to the harmonious and soothing ballads of country music. But, by far, his favorite was the soundtrack of the musical *Hamilton*.

Be Yourself, Take Your Shot

I had gone to see a performance of *Hamilton* during a retreat with my colleagues in Chicago, and when I came home and told William about it, it piqued his curiosity. He began to listen to the soundtrack — over and over again — memorizing all the words. He would sit with his oversized headphones on, playing each song on repeat, his head bobbing while he mouthed the lyrics. He was mesmerized by the rap songs that told the story of one of America's most resilient and inspiring "founding fathers." An immigrant whose hard work and perseverance enabled him to reach the highest levels of power and be instrumental in the forming of a nation, Alexander Hamilton became the perfect source of inspiration for William. His favorite song is called "My Shot." In it, the Alexander Hamilton character acknowledges the opportunity that lay before him — as well as the one that lay before a people trying to form their own nation. The song is about daring to dream big and not squandering the moment. It was an amazing metaphor for William's own personal struggle with his self-imposed limitations. It became a powerful anthem to go along with William's mantra of "Be yourself!"

One of the things I admired (and still admire) so much about William was his ability to "be himself" even when he felt nervous or self-conscious. His authenticity drew people to him. He was mature beyond his years. He was never boastful; he exuded a quiet and humble confidence. He adopted his own way to be in this world but never expected others to do things his way. He was at ease pursuing the things he was passionate about regard-less of whether he was the only one in his group of his friends doing it. He was never judgmental of other people's choices and always accepted them for who they were. This allowed others to be themselves around him. He was sensitive to what was going on with others and didn't shy away from connecting with that. At the playground, there is something called "the buddy bench" for anyone who is feeling in need of a friend. William was always willing to sit next to whoever was at the bench. His authenticity and kindness drew people to him. By being himself, he became a role model for other children — and for the adults who knew and loved him too.

• • •

To "be yourself" sounds so simple. Yet, for many of us, it is a struggle. For much of my life, I could place myself squarely in this camp of strugglers.

While the benefit of age has allowed me to more fully embrace being myself, it wasn't always the case, and it didn't come easily. It certainly wasn't the case when I was William's age. I was full of self-doubt — constantly comparing myself to others, in particular my twin brother and my father. I tried to define who I was by trying to emulate them ... because it's what I thought I should do.

There are so many pressures imposed on us by society, our families, and our peers — pressures that dictate how we "should be." These standards and expectations then infiltrate our psyche as we form beliefs about the "right" way to be in the world. After college, I pursued a career in consulting because it was how my father became successful. I thought to myself, "Do what he did, and the rest will follow." I was so seduced by the thought that I had to be a certain way to be happy that the idea of pursuing my own path never occurred to me. The inner critic in my head kept feeding me a steady diet of "You're not good enough." As a result, I became my own worst enemy — letting my fears and limiting beliefs run the show. I was so shackled by those worries and limitations that it took me another 12 years to finally consider choosing a different path. That was when William was born.

> **I was so seduced by the thought that I had to be a certain way to be happy that the idea of pursuing my own path never occurred to me. The inner critic in my head kept feeding me a steady diet of "You're not good enough."**

We all have these types of limiting beliefs and a big part of "being yourself" is about letting go of or no longer giving credence to those faulty, limiting assumptions. Letting go of those old beliefs and internal scripts requires an act of courage — the bravery to look within and challenge those assumptions and no longer be beholden to them. It requires us to have self-compassion and accept ourselves. So many times, we can do this for others (offering love and acceptance) while at the same time utterly neglecting to do this for ourselves. Finally, letting go of limiting beliefs requires that we put a stake in the ground for *who* we are and *how* we would like to be from now on. William's life was cut tragically short, but he achieved something that many are unable to in much longer lives. He made a declaration to "be himself" and followed through. He didn't throw away his shot.

> **William's life was cut tragically short, but he achieved something that many are unable to in much longer lives. He made a declaration to "be himself" and followed through. He didn't throw away his shot.**

We have this one life to live. My hope is that, by taking this glimpse into William's own journey of finding the courage to be himself, you will also be inspired to make the right choice and not throw away your shot to "be yourself." The world deserves to know you fully (and so do you).

The Resilience of the Sea

In those moments when my body felt too heavy to move,
I thought I would never be able to get up.
It would have been so simple to just lie there forever.
To shut out the world and sink into the depths
of my sadness.
That was until I saw your picture.

As always, you had that look in your eye ...
one of mischief and spirit, ready to take on the world.
At such a young age, it was the only way you
knew how to be —
like the sea that ebbs and flows with the tides.
This was the lesson you had to teach.

You gave us no choice but to endure.
Your energy and presence didn't let us quit.
Your curiosity and wonder didn't let us forget.
You taught us it was OK to keep going.
You became our guide on how to survive.

Noel

CHAPTER 11

JUST AS WILLIAM provided me with inspiration in those
darkest moments, so too did Kai. William, as the older brother, had
a big heart and loved to please. Kai, being the younger brother, was the
scrappier of the two and he was always trying to assert his place in the
world. He often uses his quick wit to challenge us in addition to making
us laugh. (Not in a bad a way, but in a way that doesn't let us off the hook.)
If we say something, he wants to know "why" and is never satisfied if we
say what all parents say: "Because we said so!" While it can be frustrating
at times to have a child so curious and strong, it is also something that
I love about Kai because he keeps me honest. We would often say that
if William was the heart of our family, Kai was the spirit. Both Susie and
I would draw on this spirit many times to keep us moving forward through
our grief. There was a specific moment when I realized this — how Kai was
helping us go on.

Kai, being silly for the camera and making his parents laugh.

One day shortly after William's accident, I was alone in our bedroom, lying on the bed. I was in one of those dark moments that had become my new default state. My depression was so heavy that I physically felt the weight of it. Every movement was an effort. I would try to get up or move and my body would just flop back down on the bed. I felt drunk or concussed and too dizzy to move in a coordinated way. The gravitational pull of my depression was too much for me; I couldn't move, nor did I want to. Many days, I had no fight in me and lying on the bed motionless provided me with just enough comfort to keep me there. Our bedroom was a place to hide … where I wouldn't have to face it all.

My depression was so heavy that I physically felt the weight of it. Every movement was an effort.

I would lie there for what seemed like hours and then have an inkling of needing to get up. I would try but to no avail. This futile battle went on for a few more cycles. Then just as I had accepted this state of isolated paralysis, my phone buzzed. Someone had sent me a text. This activated my phone from its sleep mode — and me from my semi-sleep mode — and the picture on my phone's background was a photo of Kai. He had his black Celtics hoody on with a flat-brimmed Celtics cap to match and all I could focus on were his eyes. Since the day he was born, Kai always had these huge almond-shaped eyes, and their hazel color creates a powerful mix of crystal clarity and intense depth. They draw you in. In this picture, his eyes had a look I had seen so many times before. It was one that said, "Pay attention to me. I might be the little brother, but don't you dare forget me." In that moment, it was as if Kai's image had climbed out of the phone to shake me from the fog of my depression. I had this very clear sense that I had to get up to be there for Kai. It was the first of many moments that Kai, just by his sheer nature, would inspire me to keep going.

Kai in his Celtics "fan gear."

Looking Closely, Looking Away

Kai was six years old when William died. In some ways, it was the best
possible age for something like this to happen to him. He was old enough
to have memories of his brother but not old enough to understand the
gravity of the situation. His instinct was to look for any way he could
connect to William. Susie and I were in so much pain in the days after
William's death that we had the exact opposite instinct. Any photos or
reminders of William, in those early days, were much too painful for
us. We had to look away. One day, as preparations were being made to
honor William, some friends came over to the house to help. They asked
us for a picture of William for the obituary. I gave them my phone to find
a picture and when they were finished, the phone somehow got into
Kai's hands. I looked over and saw this and noticed Kai scrolling through
the photos. My initial reaction was to take the phone away from him to
protect him from any pain. As I approached him, I was surprised to find

that he had this huge smile on his face and a twinkle in his eyes. It stopped me in my tracks.

Kai was six years old when William died. In some ways, it was the best possible age for something like this to happen to him. He was old enough to have memories of his brother but not old enough to understand the gravity of the situation.

All Kai wanted was to see his brother again. His way of grappling with this tragedy was to find new ways of connecting with William. He was showing us a different way to be, one that worked for him. He showed us how to be resilient. Over time, Kai's way of being became an aspiration for how I longed to be — able to look at a picture of William and let my love for him bring a smile to my face.

There have been so many instances where Kai's resilience has amazed me. The birth of his little brother, Bodhi, was yet another example of this. When Bodhi was born, it gave Kai the unique distinction of having been a younger brother, an only child, and older brother — all in the span of a year and a half. As always, he took it in stride. Bodhi's lung condition was another example of Kai's ability to flex. It was the height of the COVID-19 pandemic, and Bodhi's lung condition was a huge concern for our family. We were going to have to make sacrifices to protect our new baby's health. In the fall of 2020, when kids were starting to go back to school for in-person learning after five months of social distancing, we had to have a conversation with Kai about the fact that he would have to continue doing the remote-schooling option that the school provided — until his baby brother was older and stronger. There was not a single instance when Kai complained about not being in school with his friends or about our family needing to be more careful in isolating ourselves from others. He was more than happy to do it for his little brother and, as always, he did it with a smile on his face.

•   •   •

Some people have a natural aptitude for adapting to whatever life throws at them at them. Kai is one of those people. He doesn't complain; he just keeps moving forward with a positive and spirited attitude. We chose the name Kai for our second son because it was the name of one our favorite NPR hosts, Kai Ryssdal. In the Hawaiian culture, Kai means "of the sea," "from the sea," or simply "the sea." In many ways, the sea is the perfect metaphor for who Kai is. The waters of the sea are in a constant state of flux — shifting effortlessly with the tides, weather patterns, and the terrain they encounter. It is serendipitous that the significance of Kai's name is symbolic of his character. As Susie and I continued to grapple with our grief, there were countless ways that Kai became our role model, showing us that the waves might vary in intensity or speed but that we could count on them ... that time and life would keep coming at us, in a rhythm both unpredictable and soothing. By the sheer nature of who he was — a pure wave of innocence that took the shape of whatever container life poured him into — Kai signaled to us that it was OK for us to move forward.

Baby Bodhi at the beach.

Moving forward is an instinct you don't immediately have when you lose someone. My natural inclination was to associate moving forward with letting go of or forgetting William. It was an unbearable thought, but I was stuck in it; fear was preventing me from moving forward. What I realize now is that part of being resilient is about facing our fears head-on, as opposed to avoiding them. It's about how we can cultivate and hold onto the belief that, in the end, we will make it through. That is what Kai has taught me — that life is in the living, and that the only direction we can travel is forward.

Moving forward is an instinct you don't immediately have when you lose someone.

On that day, when Kai grabbed my phone and started reveling in seeing so many photos of his big brother, he was modeling for me that the only way forward is to find new ways of connecting with William. It will be painful at first, but by moving toward the pain allows us to find new ways of connecting and being. Whenever we have loss or unexpected and unwanted change in our lives, it knocks us down. The only way to pick ourselves up is to honor what *was*, accept what *is*, and embrace what *will be* with an open mind and heart. This is Kai's way, and it will serve him well as he continues his journey through life — as the little brother, the big brother, and the middle brother all at once.

Moving toward the pain allows us to find new ways of connecting and being.

Bodhisattva

You came to us to help heal our suffering,
a gift from your Big brother.
And there were times when your inconsolability
was a painful reminder of what was lost on
the way to you.

In those moments, I lost the internal battle —
allowing a shameful version of myself to emerge ...
impatient, frustrated, longing for what once was.
Woe is me. Woe is me. How can it be?

In reality, it had nothing to do with you.
This affliction has been a companion throughout,
always focusing on what could be as opposed to what is.
Samsara, as the Buddhists call it, the recipe for a life
unfulfilled.

My little Bodhi — my teacher, my son —
this is the lesson you have to offer ...
stop putting your energy in fighting the inevitable
and accept what *is* with all your heart.

CHAPTER 12

A COMMON QUESTION that people asked me and Susie in the months after William's accident was "Are you going to have another child?" Both my older sister, Caroline, and twin brother, Claude, had asked me that question on separate occasions. Both times, my answer was a resounding and emphatic "No." At 44 years old, I wasn't sure if I had the desire to go back to that stage of life — of parenting a baby once again. I love my children, but those first couple of years of a child's life can be grueling for the parents. Sleep deprivation is just the beginning. The last time I had parented a small child was almost 7 years ago. I was younger and at a different stage in my career with far less responsibility. Things were different now.

I also worried about how a new child would impact Kai. Everything was still so new and raw, and I was concerned that having another child would pull our attention away from Kai. Above all, I wanted to make sure he was going to be OK. Lastly, it just wasn't a part of the plan. You know, the plan that said: "Have kids, raise them, send them off to college, and enter the next phase of life." I am a planner and I have a hard time when things deviate from the plan. Obviously, losing a child was never part of the plan and the thought of throwing another wrench into an already unraveled plan unsettled me. It scared me.

On Second Thought

Susie always says that my first reaction to a change is "no." Despite that proclivity — and after an intense session with my therapist — I was willing to reconsider the possibility of giving Kai a little brother or sister. During that therapy session, we somehow got on the topic of having another child and my therapist made me realize that I couldn't just think of myself when making this decision. Having another child would provide an immense benefit to us all. After William was born more than nine years prior, Susie had decided to be a stay-at-home mom. William and Kai were, in essence, the focus of her life's work. And when William died, half of that focus was gone. Having another child would make her feel more whole. Susie, of course, wasn't the only one who was feeling halved, lonely, and adrift. With a new baby, Kai would have another sibling. One of the biggest tragedies when we lost William was that Kai lost his brother. This was a chance, I reasoned, not to replace William but to give Kai someone else who could be that kind of presence in his life. For me, it was a chance to be a father to another child and to do what was right for my family.

> **After William was born more than nine years prior, Susie had decided to be a stay-at-home mom. William and Kai were, in essence, the focus of her life's work. And when William died, half of that focus was gone.**

Susie and I talked it over and we agreed to try to have another child. With both of us being in our 40s, we weren't sure how long the process would take. Amazingly, as if it were a gift from William, we were able to conceive our third child after only one month of trying. When we found out we were having another boy, Susie suggested that we name him Bodhi, short for Bodhisattva. A Bodhisattva, in the Buddhist tradition, is someone who foregoes Nirvana to help others deal with suffering. This was the perfect name for our third son.

The Days Are Long and the Years Are Short

The arrival of a new baby is always chaotic, as you try to adapt to new routines and schedules. With our first two children, we had the luxury of support from family. But because Bodhi was born right in the middle of the COVID-19 pandemic, we were unable to get any additional on-site support. We were on our own.

In those initial months, Susie and I quickly settled into our different roles. For Susie, that mainly meant attending to Bodhi. My role was to take care of the household responsibilities (e.g., cooking, cleaning, grocery shopping, etc.) as well as take care of Kai. We were being ultra-careful due to Bodhi's lung condition, which meant that Kai couldn't be around his friends. I had to step in to fill that void. We played lawn games — everything from badminton, to baseball, to corn hole. It was a busy time, to say the least, juggling a full-time job along with my parental responsibilities. But I will always cherish the one-on-one time with Kai.

Like anything new, once the novelty wears off, reality sets in. This reality hit me particularly hard as Bodhi neared his first birthday. Because of the impact of the pandemic on business, I had been working hard to generate and deliver work for my company. It was early August and the last vacation I had taken was eight months earlier for the Christmas break. I was desperate for a bit of time for myself. Executive coaching work requires me to interact with people all day long. I love the work but, as an introvert, I find that extended periods of heavy interaction leave me needing time to myself to recharge. I finally decided to take two weeks off to spend time with my family on Cape Cod but was quickly reminded that being on vacation with a 1-year-old didn't present a lot of opportunities to have the much-needed "rest and relaxation" time I was craving. It was a perfect storm; the buildup of stress after two hard years — plus being overly fatigued from pushing myself too hard — all came to a head and got the best of me.

Bodhi on his 1st birthday.

I began to find myself more irritable and impatient, particularly with Bodhi. Whenever he would cry, and I was unable to quickly console him, all I could think of was how we had gotten to this point. It was a painful reminder of what we lost. I lost my oldest son and now I felt like I was losing the space I so desperately needed to stay whole. The world was closing in on me and all I wanted to do was run away. I became less helpful to Susie and any time it was my turn to take care of Bodhi, I was grumpy and resentful. Things got so bad that Susie eventually confronted me about my behavior. I lost it emotionally and, as a result, a thought — which I had buried deep down — came tumbling out. I told Susie that I had regretted our decision to have another child. The minute I heard those words come out of my mouth, I felt an intense sense of shame come over me. How could I say that about my own child? It was a moment of anger, of pain, of weakness. It was a moment I wish I could erase, that I deeply regret, and one that after much reflection has taught me a great lesson.

> I lost my oldest son and now I felt like I was losing the space I so desperately needed to stay whole. The world was closing in on me and all I wanted to do was run away.

· · ·

I have always been an impatient person, but I never considered the root of my impatience. I always chalked it up to "who I was" — that some people are hard-wired for patience, and I just wasn't one of them. Through much reflection and work with my therapist, I began to understand that my impatience with Bodhi came from longing for something I couldn't have. I couldn't have William back and I couldn't go back to how our life once was — no matter how desperately I wanted to. This tendency of longing has been an affliction of mine since I was a boy. It's the game of catch-up that I felt I had to play. When we long for something, we are always in a "waiting" mode and when we are always waiting, we get impatient. Longing also focuses our attention away from the present moment. When I got frustrated with Bodhi, I wasn't focusing on him; I was focusing on the past — on what once *was* and no longer *is*. Or I was focusing on what *will be* — a future where Bodhi is older, more independent, and where I have more free time. Neither place allowed me to enjoy the "here and now" and only created more distance between me and our new baby.

When we long for something, we are always in a "waiting" mode and when we are always waiting, we get impatient.

In the Buddhist tradition, there is a term they use to describe this sense of longing. They call it Samsara, which literally translates to "suffering." The idea is that when we form an attachment to something and then we lose it, it causes us to long for it and ultimately to suffer. Losing something is painful and I am not suggesting that we can't be with our pain and that we should suppress it. Eventually, though, the only way to move forward is to accept what is and to fully embrace it. When we fight what is — just as I was doing with Bodhi — all it does is make us unhappier. There are times where I still struggle to accept things as they are, but Bodhi is my constant reminder that when I focus on what *is* instead of longing for what *was* or what *will be*, it eases my suffering.

The Last Thought

I often wonder what he was thinking *when* ...
Were his thoughts pure and innocent like he was?
Perhaps he was reveling in the marvelousness
of the day —
the shining sun, the sky a perfect blue,
his conquest behind him, doing the thing he loved most.

Then I wonder, "What will my last thought be?"
Will it be governed by the whims of the narrator
in my head —
the one who scripts my reality but not necessarily what *is*?
He who prefers a storyline filled with worry and angst
over things so trivial and small?

If that were the case, that would be so tragic.
My last thought left to chance.
I would prefer it not to be so ...
but, rather, closer to what his was like —
pure and innocent, filled with love and wonder.

CHAPTER 13

THE POEM THAT starts off this chapter is what motivated me to write this book. When someone close to you dies, you explore death from many different angles. You put it under a microscope, trying to understand its many facets. This is particularly the case when you lose your child. You do so with the hopes of trying to connect with what the experience was like for them. What did they experience right before, during, and possibly after? You also do it to prepare yourself for the eventuality of your own death. What will it be like for me? For most of us, death is an abstract concept. It's something that lurks in the background of our lives. We know it's there, but we conveniently push it away because we can. We don't pay it much consideration.

> For most of us, death is an abstract concept. It's something that lurks in the background of our lives. We know it's there, but we conveniently push it away because we can.

As I reflected on William's experience of death, one of the things that struck me was that the moment right before he died was the very last experience he had in this life. Whatever we are doing in the days, hours, minutes, and seconds before we die, that will be our last moment of consciousness. One of the things that holds true for all of us is that our brains never stop thinking. Whether we are engaged in an activity or just vegging on the couch, thoughts run through our minds. Assuming we are conscious before we die, one of the last things we will do is have a thought.

I don't know why, but this notion captivated me, and I began to wonder how this may have played out for William. What was he thinking right before he lost consciousness? Perhaps this is just the wishful thinking of a father, but I am pretty sure that William was happy in the moments before he died. There together at Big Sky, we were in William's happiest place, his proudest place. In the second or third grade, his class did an art project creating snow globes out of construction paper and a clear plastic plate. Each child created their own personalized globe. In William's globe, there is a picture of him in his snow gear with a big smile on his face. Underneath the globe, there is written "If I lived in a snow globe ..." The idea was that each child would write their own response to that prompt beneath it. William wrote, "I would ski all day."

William's art project from school. "If I lived in a snow globe ... I would ski all day."

As William skied down the back slopes of Lone Peak, his skis crunching as he edged out his turns and the wind rushed past him, he was doing the thing he loved most with the person he looked up to the most. At just nine years old, he found his groove and his mojo after initially struggling to be at ease with himself. Out there on the slope, he was in that much-sought-after state of flow, where time seems to stop as you focus every ounce of your being on what you are doing. There was no worry and no angst, just a sense being one with the mountain and the gliding motion of his skis. He was in his snow globe. When I play all this back, I imagine his thoughts during his final moments were good. Perhaps he was replaying his glorious run or was thinking about the stories he was going to tell his friends when we got home from vacation. Maybe he was thinking about the waffle and hot chocolate I was going to get him as we reunited with Susie and Kai. Whatever the thought was, it was positive. It was happy.

Will and Kai, sipping hot chocolate.

I do believe that William died happy, and this gives me a small degree of comfort. As I try to envision what my last thought might be, I am almost envious that his was a happy one. Most of us will have no surety about when or how we are going to die, and if there is anything that I have learned from what happened to William, it is that it can happen in the blink of an eye. Here one minute, gone the next. If we can't predict when we will go, then it stands to reason that we have little control over that last thought as well. So, what will my last thought be? As I reflect on the types of thoughts I have, I realize that many of them have to do with some form of worry or limiting belief. They are governed by my insecurities and fears. It's that little voice in my head that's always telling me that I should do this or that I am not good enough. It holds me back and makes me more tentative even in the things I pursue. This voice has been so present throughout that I have felt an invisible barrier always in my way — a barrier that keeps me from showing up as my best self.

Reflecting on this, I realize that there is a distinct possibility that my last thought might not be like the one that William had but rather one that is influenced more by fear and worry. I try to envision what that would be like, and my only conclusion is that it would be tragic. It would be tragic for that to be the last thing I ever think about — for the last experience of my life to be an experience not of joy or peace, but of anxiety or stress.

•   •   •

In my work, I coach many high-performing leaders. Many of those leaders also struggle with their own set of fears and limiting beliefs. I believe that, for most of us, this is quite common. Life can be a pressure cooker — constantly forcing us to question ourselves. Reflecting upon this brings me back to why this concept of "the last thought" inspired me to write this book. We only get one shot at this life — one shot to have a last moment, one shot to have a last thought, one shot to ensure our loved ones remember us enjoying our moments and being our true selves. If you find yourself in a state where that voice in your head is not empowering but rather judgmental, self-critical, or limiting, you don't have to settle for that. Our lives don't have to be governed by fear. Those fears will always be present, but we don't have to give them the lead role.

I am not suggesting that we overthink or try to over-control our thoughts to optimize what our *last* thought will be. That would cause a whole other set of problems and, quite honestly, would be exhausting. What I am suggesting is that we don't have to accept a way of thinking that has held us back or that diminishes our happiness. We have the power to choose. We can decide to act and find the support we need to shed age-old ways of thinking, believing, and being that no longer serve us. I believe that if we can do that, we increase the probability that our last thought will be more like William's. That is my wish for you.

Epilogue

IT HAS BEEN almost five years since William died. It seems like a lifetime ago. I don't mean this just from the perspective of time but also in the sense that it feels like I have lived two lives — one with William in it and one without him. As strange as this is to say, I can't really fathom my life being any different. This is who I am. This is who we all are. Despite it all, I am happy and proud to say that my family is doing well. Susie and I have persevered through this nightmare together. All of us are doing **W**hat **W**illy **W**ould **W**ant.

We are moving forward without William in his physical form but carry his essence with us in our hearts every day. We honor and remember him always and welcome any chance to talk about him. We have adopted some new traditions that have become sacrosanct for our family. On the 19th of every month (to never forget that fateful day), we have tacos for dinner because William loved tacos. Before eating, we light a candle in his honor. We are now avid observers of the Día de los Muertos — the Mexican tradition of honoring the dead. We create an *ofrenda* (an offer in the form of an altar) that has items dedicated to William. Every year for William's birthday, I buy him a present: a Lego set that Kai (and someday Bodhi) and I build together. All of us have grieved in our own way and continue to use William as our inspiration as we move forward in this one life we have.

Susie

As Susie mentioned in the prologue, she is an extrovert, and I am introvert. My introverted way of processing everything drove me to go inward and write this book. Her extroverted way of processing everything allowed her to turn her energy outward and bring William's mantra "Be Yourself" to new light in service of an increasingly important cause: mental health. What started out as a grassroots effort by fellow parents within the Carlisle community seeking to help their children process their grief has since blossomed into a not-for-profit organization — the William's Be Yourself Challenge (WBYC). Our hope is that — through different programming and community events — we can help kids find the courage to be their authentic selves. The organization has created some wonderful events and programs in our local community and our aspiration is to broaden its reach further.

As the president of WBYC, Susie is the heart and soul that makes the organization tick. WBYC has given her an expanded purpose and a way to channel her grief for William in a positive and inspiring way. It's allowed the essence of who she is — an engaging, caring, and community-oriented person — to re-emerge after enduring the deepest pain that a mother can face. Nothing makes me happier than seeing her put her energy and passion toward ensuring the success of the organization's efforts. Seeing her smile again — just as Willy would have wanted — warms my heart.

Kai

At 11 years old and in sixth grade, Kai is doing really well. He is following his own path and honoring William at the same time. He has assembled a large collection of flat-brimmed hats, which he has neatly arranged in his room — a tribute to William. Every time he wears one (which is nearly every day), he brings his big brother with him on whatever adventure he takes. He has found comfort in sharing our story with others and can often be heard saying, "Remember that time when William ..." It's amazing to watch him grow up and find his own way through everything.

In January of 2022, I went skiing for the first time since William's accident. While it was tough to get back out there, it has provided me with a new and powerful way of connecting with William. I intend for such ski trips to become a sort of yearly spiritual pilgrimage. When I got back from my 2022 trip, Kai asked me if I thought *he* would ever ski again. I told him that it was his choice and that we would honor whatever he decided to do. A year later, in February of 2023, Kai and I went skiing at the local mountain where William used to race. During that excursion, Kai said to me that someday when he has a family of his own, he wants to ski with them. While losing his older brother will always be a part of Kai's life, he is not letting it define who he is. Kai is doing what Willy would have wanted; he is living the life that William couldn't.

Bodhi

Even though Bodhi has never met William, at three years old, he under-stands that William is a presence in our lives. In his room is a picture of William, which he gives a kiss in the mornings upon waking. He knows that William's favorite color is green. He knows that the wolf that is tattooed on my right forearm is a symbol of William. When we ask him where William is, he points his little index finger toward his heart. Bodhi has never met William but a part of me believes that their souls somehow met as William was exiting this realm and Bodhi was entering it — a brief wave from two people on opposite escalators. In many of my meditations, I try to talk to and connect with William. During one of these meditations before Bodhi was born, I asked William to tell me about his little brother. He said the following: "He's going to look like me, but he won't be me." It was another piece of sage guidance from William. Amazingly, if you look at a picture of the two of them at the same age, it's uncanny how much they look alike. The Universe works in mysterious ways.

Me

When William died, I went into a state of suspended animation as I tried to make sense of everything. You wouldn't have known it by looking at me, though, because I was able to function in a relatively normal way. At home, I was there for my family; at work, I served the needs of my clients. As an introvert, I have become quite adept at keeping hidden the storm of thoughts and ruminations that dominate my mind. I have been able to compartmentalize — to tend to the outside world when necessary and then retreat to the inside world of my mind when I need a respite. For the longest time, that inner retreat has been a place of safety and comfort — even though it hasn't always served me in the best possible way. I always tell my clients that "If you aren't uncomfortable, you aren't growing and developing." This book is me going way outside my comfort zone. It's what William wanted for me — to be myself by baring (and bearing) it all ... by writing our story so I could heal and so I could help others who are healing too.

I began writing this book in January of 2022. Since that time and through all the different cycles of editing, I have read and re-read the manuscript at least a dozen times — probably more. Every time I read *My Teacher, My Son*, I am amazed that this came out of me. It's remarkable and (even startling) what can come up — emotionally and intellectually — and what can come out — creatively or otherwise — if we let it. The stories and lessons in this book have provided me with a set of guiding principles for how I aspire to live my life. And, like all aspirations, it will require a lot of hard work and intention to achieve. That's the journey I am here to pursue. And as I do, I hope to share more of it with you.

Celebrating Bodhi's 3rd birthday. The journey continues.

My Wish for You

Our time here is brief.
So, let us not squander
all that this life has to offer.

If we open our hearts
to all that arises,
life becomes our greatest teacher.

And when moments of insight
ignite our soul,
may we share it so others can flourish.

William Wolfgang Shaw

December 20, 2009 - February 19, 2019

Acknowledgments

This book was made possible by so many people who have supported me along this journey. I feel so blessed and grateful for all who have stood by me.

My wife, **Susie Shaw** — Your strength and undying love for me and our boys has pulled me through my darkest moments. Without you, this book would not have been possible. I love you. You know I do.

My boys, **William, Kai,** and **Bodhi** — You inspire me every day to be a better version of myself. My love for the three of you knows no bounds.

The **Svatek family** — **Matt, Jesse, Eli,** and **Tori** — You have been with us since the earliest moments of our tragedy and have been by our side ever since. We are so blessed to have you in our lives.

My father, **Charles Shaw** — Thank you for loving me and my siblings fiercely and loyally in your own unique and caring way, a way that is true to who you are. Just as I know William was proud of me as his father, I am proud of you.

My mother, **Gabriela Shaw** — Thank you for being the first to believe in me and for giving me the foundation and strength to believe in myself.

My sister, **Caroline Shaw** — Your big heart and generosity have no limits. These are the gifts you bring to the world. Thank you for always being there for me.

My brother, **Claude Shaw** — we came into this world together. You have been and continue to be the Yin to my Yang. Together we are two parts of a whole that enable each other to thrive. Thank you for being you.

To **Marita Wilen** — Thank you for your unwavering love and loyalty to all of us. You were like a second mother to me, and all three of my boys love their Tatita.

To my amazing in-laws, the **Furfey** and **Gallagher** clans — Thank you for your unwavering love and support and for always allowing us to be with our grief.

To my West Coast family — the **Stubrins, Canons, Banerjees,** and **Shaws** — Thank you for holding us up and being present.

To my best and oldest friend, **Alan Shafir** — Your loyalty is unwavering and has been so since we met in kindergarten and, for that, I am so grateful.

To my partner, colleague and, most importantly, my friend — **Suki Gill** — I am so excited for this next chapter in our professional lives together to do something special. Thank you for taking the plunge with me.

To **Alvaro Silva** and **Sandra Silva** — Thank you for always opening your hearts and your home to us when we were in need. Your easy way of being provided us with so much relief when we needed it most.

To **Jim Memory** and **Katrina Baker** — Thank you for seeking out help to figure out how best to be with us in our grief and for always being there for us.

To **Laine Donell** and **Scott Donell** — Thank you for your love and hospitality and for giving us the space to be.

To my therapist and spiritual guide, **Jan Seward** — Thank you for giving all of yourself to our sessions, which gave the insight and clarity I needed to move forward.

To **Dr. Nancy Rappaport** — Thank you for helping our family heal together.

To **Jeff's Place** — Thank you for providing us with a space to connect with other parents who have suffered the unbearable loss of a child.

To my first editor, **Nina Ryan** — Thank you for pushing me to share more of my story.

To my amazing publishing coach and editor, **Kate Colbert** — Thank you for helping me to become an author. Your positive energy and uplifting spirit helped me to believe that I was capable of this.

To my book designer, **George Stevens** — Thank you for making my vision for this book a reality. Your book cover design captured the essence of everything I wanted it to be.

To **Susannah Bothe** — Thank you for taking such amazing photos of me. Your photos were able to beautifully capture me and the essence of who I am.

To the **Smith Publicity Team** — **Katie Ferraro, Courtney Link, Janet Shapiro,** and **Sandy Smith** — Thank you for your continued support in helping me do something that doesn't come naturally to me: promoting myself.

To **Curtis Staropoli** and **Killian Lennon** of **Toan Digital** — Thank you for building a website that has provided me with another medium to be able to spread my message.

To my Exetor mentors — **Graham Albutt, Shirley Grill, Donald Novak,** and **Susan Warshauer** — Thank you for always believing in me. You helped me become the coach I am today, which was critical to helping me write this book.

To **Shawna Fullington** — Thank you for your emotional and logistical support on one of the most difficult nights of our lives.

To my beta readers, **Ann Marie Tenn** and **Alessandro Martuscelli**, **Jason Burby** and **Dmitria Burby**, and **Michelle Brody** — Thank you for your honest, candid, and inspiring feedback. Your receptivity to my book encouraged me to keep going.

To **Andrea Arria-Devoe** — Thank you for encouraging me to bare more of myself in the book.

To the **ski patrollers, first reponders, doctors, nurses,** and **management team of Big Sky** — Thank you for doing everything in your power to try to save my boy's life.

To the **Carlisle Community** — Thank you from the depths of my soul for enveloping us with your love.

About the Author

Nick Shaw is an accomplished executive coach, author, and speaker known for his profound insights into personal transformation, self-discovery, and authentic leadership. Through much reflection and soul-searching, Nick has realized a need to help others find ways of living more intentional and meaningful lives. As an executive coach, Nick works with leaders to help them fully embrace the privilege of being a leader to help them create environments where their team members can thrive. Nick is the co-founder of Mirrorbox Leadership Lab, an executive coaching and leadership-development consulting firm. Utilizing an individual's real-life experiences, Mirrorbox's goal is to help senior-level leaders and executive teams bring about meaningful change in service of their personal and organizational growth.

With the 2023 release of his debut book, *My Teacher, My Son: Lessons on Life, Loss, and Love*, Nick invited readers to embark on an introspective journey of their own. Through a compelling narrative about his experience losing his son, William, at just nine years old, Nick's book stretches the boundaries of the memoir form to teach and inspire its readers and to help them through their own complex emotions and experiences. In the pages of My Teacher, My Son, Nick offers a thought-provoking and supportive guide that urges individuals to examine their lives with honesty and self-compassion. Through poignant anecdotes, Nick encourages readers to reevaluate their choices and embrace a more fulfilling and purposeful existence.

As of the publication of *My Teacher, My Son,* Nick lives in Carlisle, Massachusetts, with his wife, Susan, and his sons Kai (11) and Bodhi (3).
His eldest son, William, is buried in Green Cemetery in Carlisle, a place where the family often spends time together and finds peace. Nick and his family enjoy spending time outdoors, hiking, biking, cross-country skiing, kayaking, and stand-up paddle boarding.

William's Be Yourself Challenge

KNOWLEDGE

COMMUNITY

MOVEMENT

How can you help?

- Participate
- Volunteer
- Donate

For more information about WBYC, please contact:

Susie Shaw
President & William's Mom
Info@WilliamsBeYourselfChallenge.org

Mission

It takes courage to be yourself. The challenge is to walk your own path, to remember with joy, and to honor with love. WBYC is dedicated to community events that bring people together for authentic, meaningful connection.

Vision

We help kids find the courage to be their authentic selves

- By educating parents, teachers and kids on important mental health topics
- By providing opportunities for kids to express themselves through movement
- By building community through connection and service

Engagement

WBYC is powered by the dedication of our volunteers and financial supporters. Our goal is to reach as many children and families as possible, and with your help we can make William's mantra a reality.

BE ♥ YOURSELF

WilliamsBeYourselfChallenge.org

Go Beyond the Book

Interested in engaging Nick to speak to your audiences about key themes from the book?

🌐   Visit MeetNickShaw.com

✉   Start the conversation via Nick@MeetNickShaw.com

Ready to take your team, your organization, or yourself to the next level of leadership?

Hire Nick as your executive coach, team workshop facilitator, or leadership development consultant.

🌐   Visit MirrorboxLeadershipLab.com

✉   Every great relationship begins with "hello" — Hello@MirrorboxLeadershipLab.com

Keep In Touch

🌐 **Learn more about the book, and quickly link to all the social media channels:**

MeetNickShaw.com

✉ **Send an email:**

Nick@MeetNickShaw.com

@ **Find, follow, and share on social media:**

❶ Facebook.com/NickShawAuthor

in LinkedIn.com/in/Nick-Shaw-Author

📖 **To order books in bulk and learn about quantity discounts:**

Interested in ordering 25 or more copies of *My Teacher, My Son* for your organization, association, conference, or book club?

Inquire at Nick@MeetNickShaw.com

Printed in Great Britain
by Amazon

46039707R00089